THE KHMER ROUGE
PURGE

To: Larry, and Spencer

[signature]

4.7.26

Tom Hout Chow

THE KHMER ROUGE PURGE

*1970–1979: From Hope to Deception to Destruction: A Survivor's Story of
Cambodia's Darkest Decade*

Published by Spines

ISBN: 979-890-223-200-1

THE KHMER ROUGE PURGE

1970–1979: FROM HOPE TO DECEPTION TO
DESTRUCTION: A SURVIVOR'S STORY OF
CAMBODIA'S DARKEST DECADE

A VILLAGER'S JOURNEY THROUGH THE KILLING
FIELDS OF CAMBODIA

TOM HOUT CHOW

CONTENTS

DEDICATION

To my beloved parents,
who taught me resilience even when life
was stripped of comfort, and whose quiet
strength gave me courage to endure.
To my siblings,
scattered by war yet forever bound by love,
your silent presence on the hardest days was
a reminder that I was never fully alone.
To my villagers,
who shared food when there was none,
who watched each other's backs in the
fields,
and whose loyalty became the difference
between life and death.
And to the countless souls—neighbors,
friends, and strangers—

whose lives were cut short in the Killing
Fields,
this book carries your memory.
You are the voices that cannot be silenced,
the stories that must be told.
Above all, to my Savior Jesus Christ,
who adopted me into His family,
gave me hope when all hope was gone,
and carried me from the ashes of despair
into the promise of life.
This work is for all of you.
Your sacrifice, your love, and His grace are
forever etched in my heart.

AUTHOR'S NOTE

I did not write this book from the viewpoint of a historian analyzing distant events. I wrote it as a man who once lived through them—as a boy who watched innocence die long before he understood why.

The memories you will read were carved into me during the years when the Khmer Rouge turned my childhood into a battlefield. I cannot pretend to know every political detail or every military decision. Those belonged to others. But the fear, the hunger, the loss— those belonged to us, the villagers, the forgotten ones.

I write to honor the people whose names history does not record: the farmers who worked until their hands bled, the mothers who hid their tears, the fathers who bowed under impossible demands, and the children— like me—who learned to survive before they learned to dream.

My other books—*Out of Darkness* and *Come to Him, He's Able, He's God*—tell the story of what God did with the broken pieces that remained after the war. But this book steps back into the darkness itself, into the places where suffering first found me.

I write because their voices still cry for remembrance.

I write because truth must be spoken to guard future generations.

I write because freedom dies when people forget.

This is my testimony.

This is Cambodia's wound.

This is a reminder to the world: never underestimate the power of lies when a nation begins to believe them.

PROLOGUE

THE ASHES OF A NATION: How Deception Took Root in the Village

History often tells of wars in the language of generals and governments. It records treaties, battlefields, and dates of victories and defeats. But the story of Cambodia in the 1970s was not only written in the halls of power—it was carved into the lives of ordinary villagers like mine.

I was a boy about 11 years old in a small rural village when the storm began to rise. We lived simple lives, bound by harvests, traditions, and beliefs passed down through generations. We did not understand communism or democracy. We did not know the meaning of the Cold War. We only knew the land, the rice fields, and the rhythms of survival. To us, leaders were distant figures; their decisions were shadows on our walls, reaching us through the crackling voice of a radio, or the whispers of travelers who passed through.

And yet, it was precisely in villages like ours that deception found its strongest roots. We were uneducated, vulnerable, and too trusting of voices that promised hope. When King Sihanouk spoke from afar, urging loyalty, we obeyed. When Lon Nol declared himself protector of the nation, we listened without truly understanding. And when the Khmer Rouge came with their words of liberation, we welcomed them as saviors, never imagining they would turn into executioners.

In hindsight, it is clear how deception took hold. Our loyalty was easily won because we had so little information. Propaganda filled the gaps where knowledge was missing. Promises of equality and justice blinded us to the cruelty that lurked beneath. By the time we understood, it was too late. The Killing Fields had already been prepared—not by bombs or foreign armies, but by a regime that rose from our own soil, fueled by our trust, our silence, and our ignorance.

The ashes of a nation were not formed in a single day. They began in the quiet surrender of villages like mine —when people traded their voice for survival, when fear replaced truth, and when neighbors became enemies under orders from unseen masters.

This is the story I must tell. Not from the view of kings or politicians, but through the eyes of a boy who once believed the promises, endured the betrayal, and lived to see the cost. The Killing Fields were not only a tragedy of numbers; they were the destruction of trust, dignity, and humanity itself.

I write so that the ashes of Cambodia may speak, and so the world may never again be deceived as we were.

INTRODUCTION

The story of Cambodia in the 1970s has often been told in numbers: nearly two million lives lost, thousands of villages emptied, temples desecrated, and families torn apart. But behind every number is a face, and behind every face is a story. This is mine.

I was not a soldier or a politician. I was a boy from a small village—one of the millions of ordinary people caught between kings, generals, foreign armies, and revolutionaries. While the world debated communism and democracy, Cold War strategies and foreign policies, my life was measured in rice harvests, mosquito nets, and the cries of neighbors being led away in the night.

At first, we villagers believed the promises. King Sihanouk had been our father figure, Lon Nol claimed to save us, and the Khmer Rouge declared they would give us equality and peace. We trusted because we were simple, because we lacked knowledge, and because our loyalty was so easily manipulated. But every promise was a trap. The voices we followed into the forest became the voices that condemned us.

Deception was the weapon that struck first. It seeped into our schools, our villages, even our families. It divided us into "old people" and "new people." It turned children into spies against their parents. It taught us to distrust, to remain silent, to survive by hiding who we were. And by the time we realized, the Killing Fields were already waiting.

What I witnessed was not only mass murder, but the systematic dismantling of humanity itself. Education was forbidden, knowledge silenced, faith erased, compassion punished. Life was reduced to work, hunger, and fear. We dug canals that could not hold water, planted rice that we could never eat, and listened to endless slogans that declared we were nothing more than tools of Angkar—the Organization.

Yet even in that nightmare, seeds of resilience survived. Some hid salt beneath haystacks to feed their families. Some risked their lives to trade diamonds for a bowl of rice. Some whispered prayers in the silence of their hearts. And some, like me, carried scars but lived to tell the story.

This book is not written as history from the top down. It is written from the mud, the rice fields, the bamboo shelters, the pagodas turned into clinics, and the death pits hidden in the forests. It is a villager's story—a survivor's testimony. It is the story of how deception took root, how cruelty reigned, and how, against all odds, life endured.

I write not to relive pain, but to bear witness to it. I write for those who cannot speak, for the millions whose voices were silenced. I write for the next generation, so they may recognize the danger of false promises and the slow erosion of freedom.

And I write with gratitude—for America, which opened its doors to me when I had no home; and for Jesus Christ, my Savior, who gave me a true identity when every other name and title had been stripped away.

This is not only the story of Cambodia's Killing Fields. It is the story of what happens when lies replace truth, when ideology replaces compassion, and when fear replaces freedom. It is also the story of survival, resilience, and hope.

These are the ashes of a nation. And these are the words of one who walked through them and lived to tell.

PART ONE

FROM PEACE TO UPHEAVAL

1

UNANCHORED PEACE

KING SIHANOUK'S REIGN BEFORE THE STORM

To the world, Prince Norodom Sihanouk was many things: a king crowned as a teenager in 1941 under French colonial rule, a nationalist who won independence from France in 1953 without a bloody war, a politician who abdicated in 1955 to form his one-party movement, *Sangkum Reastr Niyum*—"the society the people love." He was also a filmmaker, a showman, and an eccentric leader who balanced Cambodia precariously between the United States, China, and the Soviet Union during the Cold War.

To us in the villages, he was none of these things. He was simply the King—our father, our protector, the man who belonged to us, and we to him. We did not know the details of neutrality or politics. We only knew he was ours.

I still remember the day in 1969, when word spread through our village: the King was coming. The whole countryside stirred with excitement. A gravel road was hurriedly laid—not for us, but so his limousine could glide smoothly after his helicopter landed. Still, we felt honored. I was about ten years old then, old enough to feel the thrill of something grand but too young to understand the politics behind it all. At school, we were told to wear our best clothes. For my brothers and me, that meant whatever simple shirts and pants my mother had carefully mended, patched, and pressed for the occasion.

It was a time when King Norodom Sihanouk was still beloved by the people, before he was later dethroned by his own general, Lon Nol. None of us could have imagined that the man we gathered to honor that day would soon be forced from power, and that our nation's future would spiral into years of turmoil and tragedy. But on that day in 1969, all we knew was joy and pride that our King was coming to our humble village.

The King's visit felt like a dream. His presence was larger than life, and even from a distance, we believed it was a sign that he cared for us. It was only after the King left that we received something more tangible—bundles of cloth dropped from the sky by helicopter, or distributed from his limousine as tokens of goodwill. The fabric was stamped with the words *Sangkum Reastr Niyum-the society the people love.* The patterns were plain, even unattractive, but to us, they were treasures. My mother stitched them into shirts for my brothers and me, and though they were simple, we wore them proudly. To us, that cloth was more than fabric—it was proof that the King remembered us.

When his limousine rolled past, women knelt, men waved their hats, and children ran alongside, shouting with joy. For those moments, we felt seen. Even the poorest among us could say proudly, "I saw the King."

But once the dust settled, life returned to what it always was: survival. Our village had no electricity, no doctors, no clean water. The school was nothing more than a roof on poles, open to the wind and rain. There were no textbooks—we copied every word from the chalkboard, and most children never came at all because their parents needed them in the rice fields.

The most dangerous time in a woman's life was childbirth. Villagers said a pregnant woman was "crossing the ocean"—no one knew if she would reach the other shore. If the baby was too large or turned the wrong way, the mother would die. No one knew how to save her. Malaria swept through the countryside, yellow fever claimed lives, and children often died before they had a chance to grow up. I lost friends to diseases I did not even understand. Few in our village lived beyond fifty.

Beneath this suffering lay a belief that shaped how we endured it: the conviction that life was reincarnated from previous lives, and that karma governed the fate of each person. If someone was born into wealth, it was thought they had earned it in another life. If someone suffered in poverty or illness, it was their karma being repaid. There was no idea of improving one's lot through learning or effort; one simply accepted whatever condition life gave. This belief was not cruel in itself—it brought comfort, a way to explain tragedy and loss—but it also dulled the desire to resist or demand better. It taught us to bow our heads, to endure silently, to wait for another life where perhaps the suffering would be less.

For many families, the hope of undoing karma rested on their sons. It was common to send boys as young as ten years old to live as monks, dressed in saffron robes, their heads shaved, walking barefoot through the villages with bowls in their hands. Some stayed only a few months, others a year or two, and a few remained for life. There was no fixed requirement—the boy himself could choose whether to return to ordinary life or continue in the monkhood. For parents, this act was seen as a way to lighten the family's burden of karma, to gain merit for the next life.

This practice was not without beauty. It reflected a deep yearning in every human heart for a better life, for hope beyond the present moment. Yet, in its cultural form, it carried both weight and subversion. For the poor, sending a son to the monastery was one of the few ways to imagine a different future. But it also meant accepting that suffering was inevitable, that justice and improvement could only come in another life.

Meanwhile, the rich remained rich. Even if they committed wrongs against the community, their wealth and position shielded them. No one dared to speak against them, for their status was considered proof of good karma. This silence preserved the cycle: privilege remained unquestioned, while the poor endured their fate with bowed heads.

For the villagers, life was a daily struggle just to meet their most basic needs. Because of their poverty and lack of education, they were treated unfairly, often taken advantage of by businesspeople who saw their desperation as an opportunity for profit. There was even a saying: *"The poor sold at a discount, the rich sold at a premium."* This saying reflected the harsh reality of the marketplace.

When villagers brought produce or fruit to sell, they had no way to preserve it. Without refrigerators or storage, they were forced to sell quickly, often at a very cheap price. Businessmen would wait until the end of the day, knowing the villagers had no choice but to accept whatever price was offered. On the other hand, when these same villagers needed to buy goods, they were forced to pay inflated "premium" prices. Their distinct village dialect made them easy to identify, and merchants exploited their vulnerability.

Even sadder was that the villagers often kept the best produce aside to sell for a higher profit, but rarely tasted the fruit of their own labor. They sacrificed their own enjoyment for

survival, trapped in a brutal cycle where poverty seemed permanent, explained away as their karma.

Every festival or celebration brought new burdens. Instead of relief or generosity, prices of necessities rose sharply. Merchants capitalized on the demand, and the government showed little concern for the plight of the poor. Special occasions, which should have been times of joy, became heavy with worry.

Later, when I came to America, I saw something very different. Here, large businesses offered steep discounts during major holidays, making it possible for both rich and poor to enjoy special occasions together. For us as refugees who had fled war and hunger, this was astonishing. In America, we felt as if we were living like the rich. We received welfare support from the government, and for the first time, we experienced the dignity of having enough. What a blessing!

Over time, I also began to notice something profound through small, ordinary moments. In my business, I often saw my employees—many of them immigrants like myself—interacting with the dentists who were our clients. In Cambodia, such meetings between workers and professionals would have been marked by distance and quiet deference. Yet here in America, something remarkable happened. When they talked about their favorite sports teams, the walls between them seemed to disappear. For a few minutes, there were no ranks, no classes—just laughter and shared enthusiasm. I realized then that even a simple thing like sports could bridge the divide between people, reminding us of our shared humanity. It was something I had never witnessed growing up in Cambodia.

When I was about eight years old, my mother once took us to visit her parents in the city. During that trip, she went to see her older sister, who was married to one of the wealthiest men there. I remember how my aunt quietly told us to stay in the back of the house because she didn't want her husband to see us. She feared he would despise our presence, believing that we, being poor villagers, might bring bad fortune to his family. Even as a child, I could feel the sting of that rejection. That moment stayed with me—it showed how deeply social class shaped our lives and how pride and superstition could wound even family bonds.

For these villagers, it was a world that longed for better but was bound by belief to wait for it rather than demand it. A society where hope was shaped by resignation, and where power passed unchallenged from one generation to the next. Looking back, I see how deeply this shaped me as a boy. It gave me patience, but it also left me vulnerable—willing to accept hardship without question, waiting for destiny instead of fighting to change it. And in that passivity, in that unquestioning loyalty, lay the seed of Cambodia's coming disaster.

Still, we adored the King. Our loyalty was unshaken because we had no other story. We did not see that in Phnom Penh (the Capitol City), the Sangkum—the society—was little more than Sihanouk's one-man rule, that corruption was spreading, that the elites who once adored him were growing restless. We did not see the communist cadres stirring in the forests, whispering of a revolution that would erase everything old to create something new.

For us, Cambodia was at peace. But it was a fragile, unanchored peace. Within a year, the King we adored would be overthrown while abroad. Our loyalty would be twisted and used to usher in a nightmare we could never have imagined. The storm was gathering, and we were standing in its path.

Deception does not arrive overnight; it creeps in through promises and propaganda. What seems harmless at first can reshape an entire people's future.

2

POWER WITHOUT VISION
LON NOL AND THE FRAGILE KHMER REPUBLIC

When I was a boy, kings did not fall. To us villagers, King Sihanouk was like the mountains—unchanging, immovable. He had given Cambodia independence, and his face smiled from posters and portraits in every school and office. We could not imagine a world without him.

So when whispers reached us in March 1970 that Sihanouk had been removed while traveling abroad, it was like hearing that the sky itself had cracked. Confusion spread quickly. Radios buzzed with strange new voices. Soldiers appeared on the roads. Neighbors argued in hushed tones, afraid of saying the wrong thing.

For us villagers, it felt like the country had lost its father and been handed to a stranger. That stranger's name was Lon Nol, the general who had seized power and declared the Khmer Republic. From that moment until April 1975, he ruled Cambodia through years of war and instability—years that slowly unraveled the peace we once knew.

He had once been one of Sihanouk's generals, a man of uniforms, medals, and speeches. In Phnom Penh, he declared a new Khmer Republic, promising to save Cambodia from communism and to stand firm with America. But his words never reached the rice fields. He governed as though the countryside did not exist, as though the only Cambodia that mattered was the capital and its officials.

Lon Nol ruled without vision because he underestimated the very people who made up most of the nation. Villagers like us were not seen as the heart of Cambodia but as a resource to be managed—a supply of young men for his army, a base of rice to feed his soldiers. He never spoke to us. He never explained why he had taken control, never gave an address to the nation to unite us. There was no effort to mend the wound left by the King's removal.

At times, I wondered if perhaps Lon Nol had tried in some way to reach out to the villagers. Maybe he sent messages through the radio or through local officials, but if he did, it never reached our hearts or changed our minds. I do not recall anyone in my village speaking well of him or feeling moved by his leadership. It seemed that whatever effort he made had little effect because the people had already made up their minds—their loyalty still rested with the King. To them, the King represented unity, identity, and blessing. Lon Nol, in contrast, was seen as a man of ambition, not compassion.

So the distance between the government and the people only grew wider. Instead of winning hearts, Lon Nol relied on military power and foreign aid, (America's) believing that control from the top was enough to hold the country together. But a nation cannot be sustained by fear and force alone. Without trust, even the strongest army stands on sand.

But Cambodia was not a country that could be ruled from Phnom Penh alone—the capital city where the King once resided and where all royal decrees and government orders flowed. The strength of the land was always in its villages—in the farmers who bent over rice paddies, in the families who lived by the cycles of planting and harvest. By ignoring us, Lon Nol weakened himself. By failing to speak with honesty and vision, he allowed doubt to take root. And by treating the King's fall as a matter of politics rather than of the heart, he failed to understand that loyalty was not won by decrees, but by trust.

His support came mainly from the cities, from those who benefited from his rise. In the villages, people felt abandoned, cut off from a leader who neither spoke to them nor cared to understand their lives. Where Sihanouk had been seen as a father, Lon Nol was a stranger—present in name, but absent in spirit.

Cambodia had been handed to a man who mistook power for leadership. He governed without fear because he believed the countryside was silent. But silence does not mean loyalty. It only means patience. And in that silence, another force was waiting, ready to speak in the voice of the King himself.

While villagers starved for answers, the communists offered something else: presence. They went into the countryside, spoke directly to the people, promised equality and food, and capitalized on the confusion and betrayal felt after the King's removal. The Khmer Republic,

weak at its core, left room for these promises to take root. Lon Nol fought not with vision but with fear, clinging to power while losing the ground beneath him.

In the end, Lon Nol himself did not suffer as ordinary Cambodians did. When his government fell to the communists in 1975, he fled the country with his family and those closest to him—those who had the means and connections to escape. They found safety in America and in places like France, far from the chaos that followed. But for the rest of his other officials who remained behind, there was no such refuge. The

Khmer Rouge came swiftly, and those who had served or supported Lon Nol's regime were among the first to be hunted down and executed.

From where we stood in the villages, it felt as though the leaders who had promised to defend the nation had abandoned it instead. Cambodia was left broken—its heart divided, its people without direction. Lon Nol's government had long been a shell, protecting itself while the countryside burned. When he fled, he left a void that the Khmer Rouge quickly filled. They did not always need to fight their way in; many villages had already been abandoned by those who should have led.

It was in this vacuum of neglect and arrogance that the Khmer Rouge tightened their grip on the countryside. They did not have to storm every village by force— often they found them already abandoned by those who should have led. Lon Nol's failure was not only in battle; it was in vision. He mistook power for leadership, and his blindness opened the door to the darkest chapter in our history.

It became clear to us, even as villagers with little knowledge of politics, that Lon Nol's downfall was not simply military defeat—it was moral failure. A leader without vision leaves his people vulnerable. A government that forgets its villages cannot expect its villages to defend it. When power becomes more important than service, and wealth more important than the people, destruction always follows.

When I look back at the Killing Fields, I cannot help but see Lon Nol as bearing a guilt of his own. Though he was not the executioner like Pol Pot, his self-indulgence in power and money, his hunger for personal gain rather than the good of the country, paved the way for ruin. In his pursuit of self-preservation, he weakened the nation until it collapsed under the weight of its own broken leadership. In this sense, his betrayal of the people made him complicit in the suffering that followed.

It became clear to us, even as villagers with little knowledge of politics, that Lon Nol's downfall was not simply military defeat—it was moral failure. A leader without vision leaves his people vulnerable. A government that forgets its villages cannot expect its villages to defend it. When power becomes more important than service, and wealth more important than the people, destruction always follows.

A leader without vision leaves his people vulnerable. A government that forgets its villages cannot expect its villages to defend it.

3
CALLED TO RESIST
THE DEFECTORS RALLY UNDER SIHANOUK'S VOICE

IN THE COUNTRYSIDE, most families did not own a radio. News traveled by word of mouth, carried along dusty roads by traders, or whispered by officials who often told us only half the truth. But my father had a large wooden radio, its frame polished with care, and in those uncertain days after the King was removed, it became a magnet for our neighbors. At night, they gathered in our home, sitting cross-legged on the floor, their faces tense, waiting for voices that might explain what had happened to our country.

The voice we longed for came at last: **Sihanouk's.**

From far away in China, his words broke through the static like thunder. He denounced the Lon Nol—self-installed illegitimate government—, and he called the people to rise against the new government. For villagers who still saw him as a father figure, his voice carried more weight than any proclamation from Phnom Penh. To us, he could do no wrong. If he said the government was corrupt, then it was. If he said the nation must resist, then we believed we must.

Yet looking back, we can see what we could not then: Sihanouk's choice of China was more than an exile's refuge—it was a political gamble with devastating consequences. If the King truly loved democracy as he claimed, then China, under Mao's Communist rule, was the most dangerous place to seek support. History now shows that by turning to Beijing for weapons and funding, he tied Cambodia's fate to a power that cared little for democracy and much for expanding its ideology. Whatever promises were made in those rooms, it was clear: to receive China's aid, Sihanouk had to give something in return. In doing so, he surrendered control of his movement, and his voice became the tool of others.

Still, the villagers never questioned his motives. To us, he remained the King who had once walked among us, the King whose helicopter had dropped cloth and gifts from the sky, the King we believed carried Cambodia's destiny in his hands. Loyalty blinded us to discernment.

We did not ask: *Why China? Why these allies? What price must be paid?* Instead, we simply listened, and we believed.

Sihanouk's words did not stop with the villagers. He urged the young intellectuals in the cities—the college students, the idealists—to flee into the forests. There, he promised, they would find people ready to help them fight. His call turned uncertainty into action. Soon, word spread that many young men had left their studies and taken to the jungle, answering what they thought was the King's command.

In our village, the effect was immediate. I saw friends, not much older than myself, volunteer to join the cause. They believed they were marching under Sihanouk's banner, fighting to restore peace and bring the King home. None of them spoke of communism. None imagined themselves as revolutionaries. They were loyal sons, convinced they were defending Cambodia by defending their King.

What we did not see was the shadow behind his voice. In the forests where the students fled, it was not Sihanouk who waited for them, but the Khmer Rouge —the communist resistance. They welcomed the recruits, trained them, and cloaked themselves in the King's name. His voice became their weapon, his popularity their disguise.

By the time Lon Nol raised his flag over Phnom Penh, he had already lost the loyalty of the countryside. The people had chosen—not out of ideology, not out of politics, but out of devotion to a King they still believed in. And in that choice, Cambodia's fate was sealed.

The pull of loyalty in our village was strong. When the King's voice called, young men felt it as a command written on their hearts. To answer was to prove themselves worthy; to refuse was to risk being seen as cowardly or disloyal—not only to the King but to their families and communities.

This was not a choice weighed with careful thought. Few paused to consider what the cost might be. The call stirred their emotions more than their reason. Many gave up their schooling, their work in the rice fields, even their dreams of marriage and family. Some went willingly to their deaths without ever asking what benefit their sacrifice would bring or whether it would truly restore Cambodia. They were swept into the tide of devotion, convinced that their obedience to the King would secure the nation's future.

What none of us could see was that this devotion was being manipulated. Behind the King's voice waited the Khmer Rouge, ready to shape this loyalty into their weapon. The young, driven by honor but blinded to the truth, became pawns in a struggle that would consume them.

Looking back, I believe even the King himself may have had good intentions. Perhaps in his heart, he truly wanted to call the people to rise up and restore

Cambodia to its past glory—to reclaim the dignity and independence that had been lost. Yet the King was not a military commander; his strength was in his influence, not in strategy or control. It is possible that while he sought to unite the nation, others around him twisted his words and used his authority for their own purpose. In that sense, he too might have been manipulated—his image and message turned into tools of deception by those waiting in the shadows.

To the villagers, however, the King's call felt noble and righteous. We followed out of loyalty and love for our land, not knowing that the very path we took in his name would lead many to tragedy. What began as devotion soon became destruction, and the movement that promised to restore Cambodia instead tore it apart from within.

In America, I have seen a different picture. Soldiers who lay down their lives are remembered with dignity. Veterans are cared for, and the fallen are buried in places of honor. Their names are engraved in stone, their graves marked with flags, their sacrifices recounted to future generations. Even in death, their service is recognized, and their families can take solace in knowing their loved ones are not forgotten.

But in Cambodia, under the Khmer Rouge, it was not so. Those who died were left in mass graves without markers, their bodies discarded as though they had no worth. There were no memorials, no honorable burials, no places where families could weep and remember. The sacrifices of the young were swallowed in silence, erased from history by the very regime that had exploited their loyalty.

This is one of the deepest wounds of our past: that the devotion of so many sons was taken, twisted, and wasted—and their memories left without dignity.

When I look back, I see how dangerous blind loyalty can be. To follow a voice without questioning its truth is to risk being led into ruin. Devotion without wisdom is like fire without control—it consumes everything in its path.

Our young men believed they were defending Cambodia, but in reality, they were unknowingly feeding the very force that would destroy it. Their sacrifice was real, but it was wasted because it was built on deception.

The lesson is clear: loyalty must always be joined with wisdom, and devotion must be guided by truth. Without these, even the most honorable intentions can lead to devastation.

4

THE WHITE KHMER REVOLUTION

FROM DREAMS OF CHANGE TO SEEDS OF TERROR

AFTER THE KING'S voice called from China, urging Cambodians to rise against Lon Nol —the new government—something began to change in the villages. At first, it was subtle—rumors whispered across rice fields, conversations carried in hushed tones at night. But soon it became visible. I remember watching streams of young men, dressed in the fine clothes of city students, passing through our village on their way into the forests. They carried themselves with determination, though some looked frightened, as if they knew they were leaving one world for another.

To us children, it was a sight of wonder more than fear. We did not understand what it meant. War was something we had only heard about in stories told by village elders—tales of ancient battles, of kings and generals long gone. We had no way of knowing that we were living on the edge of a war that would consume every-thing we knew.

Life in the village went on as if unchanged. Farmers rose with the sun, guiding their water buffalo into the fields. Mothers tended to cook. For children, we still attended school, sitting under the thatched roof, copying words from the chalkboard because we had no books. Outwardly, the rhythms of daily life continued. But beneath that rhythm, there was a growing tension, like the stillness before a storm. We could feel some-thing was shifting, though we did not yet have words for it.

What unsettled us most was how the King's tone had changed. To us, Sihanouk had always been a father of peace, the smiling figure who waved from his limousine and dropped bundles of cloth from the sky. But now his voice carried the urgency of war. He called not for harmony but for rebellion. He declared that Lon Nol had betrayed him, selling himself to the Americans, and that the only way to save Cambodia was to take up arms.

The villagers believed him. They were naïve, perhaps, or simply too uneducated to question what they were told. But loyalty to the King ran deeper than logic. If he said Lon Nol was a traitor, then he was. If he said resistance was the path to salvation, then that became the truth. For people who had never studied politics or read books, the King's voice was an unquestionable authority.

Even I, a young boy, absorbed those words without understanding. I could not yet imagine what war meant. I only knew that something irreversible was beginning. The King was far away in China, but his words carried through the forests, gathering followers in his name. No one anticipated who would truly lead this revolution. No one realized that in following the King's call, we were placing our future in the hands of others who would twist his words into something far more dangerous.

In those early days, it was still called the "White Khmer" revolution—a movement that promised purity, justice, and renewal. But hidden within it were seeds of terror that would soon take root. We did not see them then. We only saw the King's shadow and believed we were walking in his light.

The White Khmer Illusion

Looking back now, I realize how blind we villagers were to the meaning hidden in names. When we first heard of the **"White Khmer"**, it did not alarm us in the least. White, to us, meant purity, peace, and hope. It was a color associated with honesty, with beginnings, with something good. We welcomed the name. It gave us a sense that this movement was something noble, even protective—an extension of our own culture and values.

But names carry power, and names can deceive. Slowly, without announcement or explanation, the "White Khmer" faded away, replaced with a new name whispered first, then declared openly: **the Khmer Rouge.**

For us villagers, it seemed like nothing more than a small change in words. But in reality, it was the signal of something much deeper. "Rouge"—red—was not just a color. It was a symbol of blood, of revolution, of the Marxist ideology creeping in from beyond our borders.

Where "white" had promised purity, "red" demanded sacrifice. Where "white" suggested peace, "red" pointed to struggle and violence.

We had no choice in this transformation. The name was changed without our approval, without even our understanding. We did not know that by the time we accepted the Khmer Rouge into our villages, the seeds of terror had already been planted. The white mask of purity had only been a disguise, a cover to win the loyalty of the people. Once recruitment had been fulfilled and the movement had grown strong, the mask was thrown aside, and the true face began to emerge.

What made us accept this so easily was not just igno-rance—it was loyalty. We had already pledged our hearts to the King's voice (as I shared in the last chap-ter). When Sihanouk, from far away in China, urged the people to resist Lon Nol and join the fight, we believed we were answering his call. If he said these young fighters were our defenders, then we trusted them. If he said they were for the people, then we welcomed them.

That loyalty gave the "White Khmer" credibility they did not earn. We never asked what they truly believed. We never questioned their motives. To us, they carried the King's blessing, and that was enough.

But looking back, I see now how dangerous blind loyalty can be. China was no place for a democracy-loving King to seek refuge—it was a communist strong-hold. And if China supported him, it was not without cost. Military equipment and funding always come with a price. The King's name, his influence, his people—these were the bargaining chips. And in the end, he lost control of the very movement he had unin-tentionally endorsed.

The villagers could not see this. We only heard his voice, still calling us from the radio, still urging resis-tance. We believed we were serving the King, when in truth, we were feeding the rise of the Khmer Rouge. Our loyalty without discernment, our trust without question, became the very path that led us into destruction.

The White Khmer became the Khmer Rouge.

The voice of the King became the weapon of the revolution.

And the devotion of the people became the chains that bound them.

5
BROTHERS IN ARMS
NORTH VIETNAMESE SOLDIERS ENTER CAMBODIA

THE KING WAS GONE, but his voice was everywhere. Broadcast from Beijing, his words carried more power than his presence had ever done in the villages. We seldom spoke his name before, but now his voice commanded us like thunder rolling through the forest. He called for resistance, and people listened. Yet beneath that loyalty, some began to whisper. Why China? Why align himself with Mao's communists?

My father was among those who questioned. He had been born in China and fled to Cambodia during the turmoil of Mao's rise. Like many Chinese who scattered across Asia—settling in Vietnam, Thailand, Laos, Singapore, and Cambodia—he had left his homeland behind and never saw his family again. He knew the nature of war, and he knew the cruelty of communist movements. When he heard the King's voice calling from Beijing, he warned us that difficult days were ahead. But I was a boy, and naïve. To me, the world still seemed simple, though change was closing in fast.

In the countryside, people clung to the hope that the "White Khmer" would restore the King and drive out Lon Nol. They were seen as rescuers, fighting against an illegitimate government. We believed they wanted only to give Cambodia back to her people. It all seemed noble enough—until the morning the war walked into our village.

I still remember it clearly. A group of about fifteen men on motorbikes rolled in from the forest. They introduced themselves as Viet Cong—North Vietnamese soldiers. They carried rifles we had never seen before: the AK-47, a weapon made in China. They spoke with confidence,

unafraid and calm, as though the land already belonged to them. They smiled, greeted villagers, and even joined us for breakfast, sitting on the floor and eating rice as if they were old friends. Then they explained why they had come. They were here to lead the fight. They were experienced soldiers, trained and armed, ready to help the White Khmer take control of the territory.

After eating, they rode toward the highway—the road that connected us to the great city of Siem Reap— known as the Angkor Wat. Later that day, we heard the news: the Viet Cong had ambushed Lon Nol's soldiers. About twenty government troops who guarded the post were killed. In one strike, the main highway no longer belonged to Lon Nol. That day, the war in Cambodia had truly begun, and without realizing it, we villagers had become enemies of the Republic.

Not long after, the Viet Cong began to station themselves among us. Cambodian houses were built high on stilts, with open space beneath for cows and chickens. The soldiers moved into that space, hiding in groups of ten or so, using us as their cover against Lon Nol's spies. This made the villagers uneasy. These were our homes, our families' shelters, yet suddenly soldiers were living beneath us. We could not simply leave; the houses were our lives, built by our fathers and grandfathers. Now they had become shields for foreign soldiers.

Only later did I understand why our village was so important to them. We lived at the edge of a vast forest, dense and nearly impossible to penetrate. That jungle stretched one way toward Vietnam and the other toward Thailand. It was more than trees—it was a secret corridor, a hidden highway that connected armies and supplied revolutions. For soldiers, it was priceless. Whoever controlled that forest controlled the arteries of war.

To us, it was just home. The forest was where we gathered firewood, where children hunted birds with slingshots, and where fathers cut bamboo and trees for building. We thought of it as a place of life. But to the Viet Cong, it was a place of war. Our village, sitting at its edge, was the doorway. They could come in and out with ease—vanishing into the jungle when danger came, reappearing when it was time to strike.

At first, their presence seemed polite, even respectful. They greeted our elders, shared meals, and paid for the dogs they ate. And yet even in their courtesy, there was unease. For

For Cambodians, dogs were companions, guardians of the home, partners in hunting. To see them treated as meat was disturbing, even offensive. It reminded us that these men, though allies, were not like us. They lived under our houses, ate our food, and fought in our fields, but their ways were foreign.

Meanwhile, the radio broadcasts began to change. At first, all we heard was the King's voice. But gradually new names were introduced—Khieu Samphan, Heng Samrin, Son Sann. These voices spoke as though they were in command. The King's name appeared less and less, until at times it vanished entirely. In the village, we assumed he had delegated his authority to loyal lieutenants. We did not realize his influence was already slipping away.

By then, Cambodia was already divided. The cities belonged to Lon Nol, his government propped up by American money and soldiers patrolling the main highways. But the countryside—the villages, the rice fields, the forests—was under the control of the revolution. With the Viet Cong by their side, the Khmer revolutionaries claimed more territory each day. For villagers like us, there was no middle ground. We were not asked which side we wanted. By living in the countryside, we were already counted as part of the revolution.

It was as if the country had split in two: one Cambodia dressed in uniforms, holding parades in Phnom Penh; the other hiding in forests, eating rice from bamboo bowls, and planning ambushes under our stilted houses. And we villagers, caught between them, had no choice but to live with the side that had come to stay.

When the North Vietnamese soldiers—whom we called the Viet Cong—first appeared in our villages, they did not come with fanfare or flags. They slipped quietly into our lives, setting up camps in the forests, using our rice fields and streams, and eventually moving under our very homes. At first, we thought it was a temporary arrangement, just a hiding place before they moved on. But as the war deepened, their presence became part of our daily reality.

They were disciplined, organized, and always seemed to know when danger was near. To the villagers, they were at once intimidating and strangely familiar, eating our food, sleeping in our barns, sharing our spaces. For some, they even offered protection. Yet their presence carried a cost far greater than we realized.

Looking back now, I understand more clearly why the Viet Cong stayed so close to us—not only to avoid spies, but to use us as **human shields**. By sleeping under our houses and moving among our families, they made it nearly impossible for Lon Nol's soldiers—or later, the Americans—to strike at them without also striking us.

At the time, we did not see it this way. We were simple villagers, trying to survive. But unknowingly, we had become part of the battlefield. By hosting them, even involuntarily, we were branded as accomplices. On Lon Nol's lists, there was no distinction between a Viet Cong soldier and the farmer whose house he occupied. To the outside world, we were one and the same— villagers aiding the enemy.

This was the nightmare we lived: trapped between two sides, blamed by both. If Lon Nol's troops came, they would accuse us of harboring communists. If we resisted the Viet Cong, they could punish us—or worse. Our homes, once a place of safety, became prisons of fear.

For us children, it was confusing and terrifying. We did not know who was right or wrong, only that our village was now a chessboard where bigger powers moved their pieces. The line between friend and enemy blurred until it disappeared.

How could Lon Nol's soldiers tell who was Viet Cong and who was a villager? They could not. And so, when bombs fell, innocents suffered alongside fighters. We had no way to clear our names, no proof to separate ourselves from those who used our roofs for cover.

What the Viet Cong saw as strategy, we experienced as suffering. What seemed clever in their war against Lon Nol and the Americans was, for us, a nightmare that stole our peace, our security, and too often, our lives.

6

A NEW NAME

A DARK PATH

THE WHITE KHMER revolution had begun with the King's call, a promise of rescue and restoration. But soon, something changed. New rules were announced, not as suggestions but as orders. The rice fields, once owned by families, were no longer ours. They belonged to the community. Only

the house you lived in remained "yours," but everything else—the land, the tools, the harvest—was said to belong to *Angkar.*

No one knew exactly what *Angkar* meant. It was a word spoken with authority, a shadowy power above us all. When the order came, it was not explained. We were told simply to obey—because *Angkar* had spoken. To question was unthinkable.

In truth, *Angkar*—which means "the Organization" in Khmer—was the secret name used by the Khmer Rouge leadership. To us villagers, it was mysterious and faceless, an unseen hand that decided everything. *Angkar* decided who lived and who died, who ate and who starved, who was loyal and who was an enemy. Yet no one ever saw *Angkar*. Its presence was everywhere, but its form was nowhere. Even local cadres claimed they did not fully know who *Angkar* was. That mystery was part of its power.

We whispered the word, half in fear and half in ignorance, not knowing whether it meant a person, a council, or something else entirely. But one thing was certain—*Angkar* had become our god and our judge. Its voice came through soldiers, slogans, and loudspeakers, replacing the voices of family, religion, and reason. All we knew was that our lives no longer belonged to us.

Then came the new name. For the first time, the revolution was called the Khmer *Rouge*. To us villagers, the phrase meant little. It was foreign, a label that sounded strange and heavy in our ears. But those who used it told us it meant strength, unity, war. We were told Cambodia was in a great battle, and the frontlines needed food, supplies, and loyalty. Every family, every person was part of that fight. It sounded noble enough, and many believed it. What harm could there be in giving rice for the soldiers, in working harder for the nation? But beneath the name was a harder truth. The

Khmer Rouge was not simply a movement of loyalty to the King—it was a communist party, unfamiliar to us, reshaping the nation in ways we could not yet understand.

Alongside these changes came new punishments. At first, they seemed small, almost laughable. Men who drank too much rice wine—once only pitied or scolded by neighbors—were now arrested. Their hair was shaved off, and a wooden plaque was hung around their necks with words like: *"This is the model not to follow."* They were paraded through the village as examples of shame. We children, whispered and giggled nervously, not knowing whether to laugh or to be afraid. Our parents watched in silence. This was something new, something unsettling.

Looking back, I see that these punishments were the beginning of a system built on fear. No one was executed yet, but humiliation was enough to teach obedience. The revolution was showing us that nothing, not even small vices, would be tolerated. Fear crept into daily life, and villagers

began to watch their own behavior carefully, not out of conviction, but to avoid becoming the next example.

Then the war crashed into our lives with fire from the sky. One morning, two fighter planes roared over our village. We had little warning before the bombs fell.

They struck our elementary school, leveling every building to the ground.

Our school had never been grand—wooden walls, thatched roofs, open spaces to let in sunlight—but it was ours. It was the only place where children like me could hope to learn something beyond the rice fields. In a single strike, it was gone. Dust and splinters filled the air. The sound of children's voices, once echoing through the open classroom, was silenced.

The surrounding trees were torn apart, their branches hanging like broken limbs. Coconut trees that once lined the path stood cut in half, like candles after a storm—but this was no celebration. It was a day of mourning, the first great loss our small hearts had ever known.

That day, school ended for us. Childhood ended, too.

When the roaring faded and the dust began to settle, the village fell into a stunned silence. Mothers ran toward the ruins, calling the names of their children, their voices breaking with fear. Fathers dug through the wreckage with bare hands, searching for any sign of life. The air smelled of smoke and earth. Even the animals were quiet—as if the whole world had paused to grieve.

I stood frozen, unable to move. The ground still trembled beneath my feet. My mother's hand found mine, trembling, and she whispered, "Let's go home." On the way back, I looked around and saw our familiar paths torn apart—trees splintered, roofs caved in, the rice fields pockmarked with craters. It felt like the earth itself had been wounded.

That night, no one in the village slept. We gathered in silence, our faces lit only by flickering oil lamps. Some wept softly; others stared into the darkness, wondering if the planes would return. In our hearts, something had changed forever. The world we knew—the one filled with laughter, lessons, and the sound of children reciting their lessons—was gone.

From then on, we were told to dig shelters. Every family was responsible for their own. My family dug ours beside the river near our house, hidden among the bamboo bushes. We carved out the earth with hoes and bare hands, lining it with bamboo poles and wood for support. It became our refuge when the planes returned, a place of darkness and fear. The war was no longer a rumor or a voice on the radio. It was above our heads, under our feet, pressing into every breath we took.

What deepened the wound was what we heard afterward. The next day, Lon Nol's radio broadcast declared that an operation in our village had succeeded. They reported that Viet Cong weapons had been destroyed and many casualties inflicted. We listened in disbelief. There had been no weapons, no soldiers, no battle—only our wooden school, shattered into the ground. For the first time, we realized the government was not simply losing the war. They were lying about it. From that day forward, every "victory" they reported was heard with suspicion. In their voice, we no longer found truth—only propaganda.

The name *Khmer Rouge* grew louder in the days that followed. It was no longer just a word—it was the banner under which the countryside lived. We did not know the full meaning of it then. We did not know how deep its darkness would go. But we were already living in its shadow, and the path we walked was no longer one of dreams but of survival.

What made the Khmer Rouge so effective was not their open force, but their quiet calculation. They did not begin by demanding sacrifice. They began by cleaning up what villagers already resented—the drunkards who stumbled through markets, the bandits who stole from families, the men whose reckless behavior had long been a burden to village life. When these people were suddenly dealt with, the villagers saw it as justice. It seemed as if the newcomers cared about the welfare of the community, about protecting ordinary families from disorder.

By doing this, the Khmer Rouge won trust without stirring suspicion. They appeared as guardians of morality and order. They spoke softly of unity, discipline, and a better future. What they never revealed was the cost they would later demand. Every act of "protection" was a rehearsal for control. Every promise of safety was a step toward domination. And every villager who felt grateful in those early days was being drawn, unknowingly, into a web of sacrifice for a war they did not choose.

Life in the village had never been easy, even before the war. We had lived day to day—planting, harvesting, and trading what little we had to survive. But now, even that fragile rhythm was shattered. The war reached into every corner of our existence. Roads that once led to the city were cut off; markets fell silent. Supplies of salt, medicine, and cloth disappeared. Families who relied on selling their crops could no longer trade. Hunger crept in quietly, and fear became our daily companion.

We were cut off from the outside world, from the flow of goods, news, and hope. Each sunrise brought uncertainty—would soldiers arrive? Would there be fighting nearby? Would our sons be taken? What had once been hardship now became something far heavier: a fight simply to stay alive.

We were no longer just villagers. We were people caught in a storm we could not escape. The country was at war—and whether we understood it or not, we were all already part of it.

War does not always arrive with warning. Sometimes, it slips quietly into the corners of ordinary life—until one morning, you wake to find the world you knew no longer exists. That was how it came to us. One day, we were farmers and traders; the next, we were survivors.

The sound of gunfire became the new language of the land. Rumors replaced truth. Trust, once the strength of our villages, began to fade as fear took its place. Every path seemed dangerous, every stranger a threat. We longed for peace, but peace had already fled from us.

The old Cambodia—the one of laughter in the rice fields, of children running barefoot under the palm trees, of families sharing stories by the fire—was slipping away. In its place rose a new world built on suspicion, obedience, and silence. We did not yet know the full weight of what was coming. But deep inside, we could feel it: the ground beneath our feet was shifting.

The war had reached our doorstep. And from that moment on, nothing would ever be the same.

PART TWO

FIELDS OF FIRE

7
DRAFTED INTO DARKNESS
RECRUITMENT AND FORCED CONSCRIPTION

THE DAYS of asking for volunteers were gone. By now, Angkar no longer persuaded—they commanded. When the cadres came to our village, their orders were simple: every boy aged fourteen and older must join the army. It did not matter if you were in school, if your family needed you in the fields, or if you were still a child in your mother's eyes. Angkar had spoken, and that meant the matter was closed.

One by one, my childhood friends were taken. Some tried to hide in the forest, but it never worked for long. Others went quietly, their faces pale but determined, believing it was their duty. Many of them never came back. Some were killed in battle, others vanished into the revolution, consumed by a war that was no longer about the King but about survival. For their families, there was no grave to mourn, only silence and unanswered questions.

My brothers and I were spared, but not by choice. Because we were ethnic Chinese, we were told we could not be conscripted unless we volunteered. It was a strange kind of exemption—on one hand, it saved us, but on the other, it set us apart. We were still watched, still suspected, as if our blood made us less loyal to the cause.

One of my cousins was also Chinese like us. He did not have to join—but he volunteered. Perhaps he believed the words of the cadres, or perhaps he simply wanted to prove that he belonged, that he was just as loyal as anyone else. I could not say anything to stop him. To resist would have been to question Angkar, and to question Angkar was unthinkable. I watched him leave with the others, his back straight, his face unreadable. He walked out of the village that day, and I never saw him again.

For those of us left behind, Angkar gave no freedom—only a different assignment. We were grouped into units of five families, each given a portion of rice fields to cultivate. Our duty was not to fight with guns, but to fight with labor. The rice we grew was not ours to keep; it was

for the revolution, for the soldiers at the frontlines. The

land became our battlefield, and the harvest our weapon.

The cadres framed it as a duty. They told us the front-lines needed strength, that the enemy was closing in, that young men must prove their loyalty by fighting. But beneath their words was a simple truth: the revolution was eating its own children. It no longer mattered what you believed, whether you supported the King, Lon Nol, or no one at all. If you were of age, your life was no longer yours. It belonged to Angkar.

For us who remained, every visit from the cadres filled us with dread. Mothers clutched their sons tightly, hoping to shield them, but nothing could protect them from the lists carried by the recruiters. Fathers bowed their heads in silence, powerless to defend the children they had raised. The sound of footsteps approaching the village became the sound of fear itself.

Looking back, I see that this was the moment when the revolution revealed its true face. What had begun as a call to defend the King had become a machine that devoured the young. Hope of restoration was gone. In its place was a darkness that pulled us deeper every day, leaving us with only two choices: obedience or disappearance.

Laughter Beneath the Bombs

Even in the rice fields—once a place of sweat, laughter, and harvest—the shadow of death followed us. We worked under the burning sun, our hands raw from the mud, our backs aching from endless labor. Every strange noise in the sky made our hearts freeze. Sometimes it was just the wind, or a bird's cry, but other times the sound came like a deep rumble—foreign, metallic, and terrifying. We never knew if it was thunder or warplanes. And we could not take chances. At the first echo, we dropped our tools and ran for the bomb shelters, tripping over one another in panic.

When the air fell silent again, we would crawl back out, shaking, confused, and ashamed. The cadres would mock us for our fear, accusing us of weakness or superstition. They said the brave ones stayed in the fields, that the revolution had no place for cowards. But they did not understand—it was not just the sound of bombs we feared; it was the sound of death itself, echoing in our ears day and night.

Yet the louder fear was not from the skies—it was from within. The name *Angkar* carried a weight greater than any explosion. It was a name whispered but never questioned, feared but never seen. We knew they were ruthless, willing to sacrifice countless lives for their vision of victory. To disobey was to vanish. To speak was to die. And so, we worked, we bowed, we pretended to believe, even as our souls trembled inside.

What a life we lived—half in the open, half in hiding. Our bodies labored in the fields, but our hearts were prisoners of fear. Between the war above and the terror below, there was no safe ground left to stand on. Only the will to survive kept us moving, one uncertain day at a time.

And yet, even in that darkness, we found moments that made us laugh—small bursts of humor that eased our pain. After the bombs had fallen and the smoke cleared, we would sometimes discover neighbors tangled in thorn bushes, crying for help because they had thrown themselves into the nearest hiding place without looking. We had to cut through the branches with machetes to free them, shaking our heads and wondering how they managed to get in so deep. It happened more often than one might believe. Perhaps fear gave them the strength—or the foolishness—to dive where no person should fit.

Then there was the father and his young son, who were running late to the bomb shelter. When the planes came, he grabbed his boy and leapt into the slow-moving river nearby. Each time a bomb dropped, he would push his son and himself underwater, believing the water would shield them from harm. It was a strange, desperate instinct—but when we later told the story, we laughed until our sides hurt.

Looking back, those moments of laughter were not mockery—they were medicine. In a world ruled by terror, laughter was proof that our souls still lived. It was our quiet rebellion, our reminder that even fear could not completely steal our humanity. In the midst of bombs, hunger, and death, we still found ways to smile. And sometimes, that was enough to keep hope alive.

8

FIELDS OF FIRE
BOMBING THE COUNTRYSIDE

THE BOMBINGS BECAME a part of daily life. At first, the planes had targeted structures—roads, bridges, posts guarded by soldiers. But soon, the strikes grew more intense. The planes did not only bomb buildings; they strafed the fields, firing at anyone who could not reach shelter in time. Villagers—men, women, and children —were cut down in the open. Innocent lives were lost almost daily.

What troubled me most, even as a boy, was how the Viet Cong seemed to know in advance what would happen. They would tell us how many planes would come, at what time, and where the bombs would fall. They urged us to leave our village, warning that it was no longer safe. But they did not understand—this was our home. Our houses, our rice fields, and our ancestors' graves were here. Where could we go? Even when we believed their warnings, there was no refuge. Every direction led to the same danger. So we stayed, hiding in the bomb shelters, waiting for the planes to come, praying that somehow the earth above us would hold.

And every time, it happened just as they said. The planes came. The bombs fell. Our village shook. Our lives were scattered. What puzzled me even more was how calm the Viet Cong soldiers were. The bombing seemed to be nothing more than a routine to them. Before the attack, they would gather, sometimes sharing food and laughter as though celebrating some secret victory. Then, almost casually, they would move away to a safe place, never in haste or panic. When the skies cleared and the smoke lifted, they would return, stepping over the ruins as if nothing had happened.

After witnessing this several times, my curiosity grew. I could not understand how they always knew. One day, I gathered the courage to ask one of the soldiers. He told me they had a listening device that alerted them when planes were coming. But I did not believe that was the whole truth. There had to be something more —something I could not comprehend at that time. It felt as if they were following a script written in advance, and we were the ones left behind, helpless actors caught in a story of destruction we never agreed to play in.

In those moments, I learned a lesson that would stay with me for life: that not every warning is meant to protect you, and not every silence means safety. The war taught me early that trust could be dangerous, and fear could be a teacher. Even as the bombs fell, I realized that survival was not just about running or hiding —it was about learning whom to believe, when to move, and when to stand still in the face of uncertainty.

But the Khmer Rouge did not have the same knowledge. One day, planes struck the Buddhist temple where Khmer Rouge soldiers were stationed. They had no warning. When the attack came, many of them were killed instantly, and others were badly wounded. I still remember the sight of their bodies carried away, their blood staining the steps of a sacred place. For the first time, I realized that even the revolutionaries were not invincible. The Viet Cong seemed always one step ahead, but the Khmer Rouge—who lived among us, who claimed to be our protectors—were just as vulnerable as we were.

As a child, I could not understand it. Later, when I came to America, I searched for answers. I learned that American bombers were stationed not in Cambodia, but across the border in Vietnam. How much more there was behind it, I do not know. What I do know is this: for us in the villages, the bombs were real, the wounds were real, the fear was real. And no explanation from any side could undo the destruction that became part of our daily lives.

For villagers like us, it was too much. We were people of simple lives. We planted rice, raised our children, celebrated the new year with dancing and drums, and told folktales by the fire. Life was not easy, but it was pure. Innocence was our way of surviving. Now that innocence was shattered. We were being asked to endure things far beyond what our hearts could carry.

The bombs made us feel small, powerless, and hopeless. They came from the sky without warning, unstoppable, indifferent to whether they struck soldiers or children. Every time the earth shook, every time the bomb shelters rattled over our heads, a piece of our trust in the world collapsed. Fear was not just in the moment of attack—it stayed with us afterward, in our sleep, in our daily work, in the silence between raids.

Every raid ended the same way: with us running toward the wounded. We carried those who could still be saved into the forests, where Angkar had set up hidden shelters. There, in crude huts or beneath the trees, they tried to care for the injured with whatever medicine or

knowledge they had. Bandages were made from cloth, and wounds washed with water from the streams. It was far from enough. Many died on the way. Many more suffered in silence. This became our routine: to dig, to hide, to run, to carry.

The destruction left behind was everywhere. The surroundings of our village became a silent testament to what we had endured. We were too busy hiding and running to repair what was broken. Coconut trees stood snapped in half, jagged and bare, like giant candlesticks mourning the violence that had cut them down. Tree limbs dangled and splintered, scarred in ways no one could ever repair. Fields were gouged open by craters, houses shattered into piles of bamboo and thatch. The earth itself seemed to grieve. Even now, I cannot fully comprehend the scope of the damage. It was more than physical—it was a wound to the soul of the village.

And slowly, that fear began to push us into Angkar's arms. They were the only ones who seemed to offer protection, the only ones who spoke with certainty, who gave instructions on where to dig, where to run, how to survive. We did not trust them fully, but who else was there? Lon Nol's government was far away, hiding in the cities, lying about victories that never happened. The King was in China, his voice growing fainter with each passing month. Only Angkar stood among us, present in our villages, speaking with authority, shaping our lives.

Innocent as we were, we clung to them—not out of loyalty, but out of desperation. For people who once lived simple, pure lives, it was more than we could bear. And so, without realizing it, we allowed fear to lead us deeper into the darkness.

9

SALTLESS TEARS

VILLAGERS' SILENT SUFFERING
WITHOUT MEDICINE OR AID

THE WAR HAD DIVIDED Cambodia into two worlds. In the cities, Lon Nol's government held control, where supplies and household goods were manufactured and distributed. In the countryside, the Khmer Rouge dominated, but they had no factories, no trading companies, no way to produce anything beyond rice. And so, though they claimed to be building a new nation, the reality was stark: villagers like us were cut off from even the simplest necessities of life.

Medicine was the greatest loss. There were no clinics, no doctors, not even a place to buy aspirin or Tylenol. For generations, villagers had depended on the *kru khmer*—the medicine man—who used herbs gathered from the forests. Sometimes his remedies worked, but more often they only eased the pain for a while. They could not cure malaria, yellow fever, or the stomach worms that plagued almost every child in the village, myself included. Disease swept through our homes like a tide, and we were powerless to stop it.

Even our animals suffered. Every summer, when the heat grew fierce and the rains delayed, disease spread quickly among the chickens. One bird would fall ill, then another, until the whole flock seemed doomed. It did not pass to humans, but it robbed families of precious food. We learned to slaughter the chickens early, to eat them before the sickness overtook them completely. At the time, we accepted it as part of life, another hardship to endure. Later, when I came to America, I heard of "SARS" and other epidemics, and I realized what we had faced was not just misfortune, but part of a larger truth: in times of weakness and neglect, even nature itself seemed to turn against us.

There was another sorrow we rarely spoke of, though it was common in the village: the number of babies born with deformities. Some came into the world with twisted limbs, missing fingers, or other defects we could not explain. To us, steeped in the old beliefs, the explanation was simple. These children were reincarnations of soldiers who had died in war—men and women who had lost arms, legs, or lives on the battlefield, now reborn into bodies marked by their past. Villagers accepted it quietly as fate, as karma working itself out.

But looking back now, I cannot help but wonder if it was something else. The endless bombings, the explosions that shook the earth and filled the air with smoke and chemicals—could they have poisoned the soil and the mothers who lived on it? Could the war itself have etched its scars into the bodies of the children yet unborn? At the time, I did not know. I only knew that life in the village was fragile, that suffering came not only in hunger and sickness, but in the very births of our children.

The absence of salt was another silent enemy. Without salt, the body could not stay balanced. People's legs and faces began to swell with water. If you pressed a finger against the skin, it left a hollow mark, the body unable to release what it held. For the poor, this suffering was a daily reality. My family was fortunate— my parents had hidden a supply of salt, saved quietly for us. But for many others, there was nothing. Salt became more valuable than gold, and its absence ate away at the strength of the people as surely as disease did.

By 1972, my father became gravely ill. We had no hospital to take him to, no doctor to call, no medicine beyond what the *kru khmer* could offer. We watched helplessly as his health failed, his body weakened by years of hardship and now by sickness that no herb could heal. Within a year, he was gone. He was only fifty-four years old.

His death broke something in me. My father had left his home in China as a young man, seeking freedom and a new life in Cambodia. He had escaped one revolution only to end his days in the shadow of another. Just before he passed away, I remember him saying words that seemed strange at the time: *"Eat what you can now, because in the future you will not have the privilege to eat like you used to."* As a boy, I did not fully understand what he meant. But later, when hunger and deprivation tightened their grip on us, his words returned with haunting clarity.

Still, the villagers were resilient. They refused to give up, even in the face of disease and hunger. I remember how they watched the birds. Flocks would gather on certain bare patches of ground to peck at the soil. These places were different—the grass and plants would not grow there, for the earth was rich with minerals. The villagers took this as a sign. They joined forces to dig deep wells in those spots, drawing up water that had a faint salty taste.

The work was exhausting. Buckets of water had to be carried home and boiled all day long just to produce a few grams of residue. Yet this tiny amount was precious. They called it the "miracle salt." Families who had nothing else now had at least a trace of what their bodies needed. It was never enough, but it was something. Looking back, I realize it was survival born of desperation and of hope—the determination of ordinary people to fight for life with whatever nature provided.

Even so, disease struck hard. I myself fell victim to malaria. The attacks came daily, almost with the precision of a clock. First came the violent chills that shook my body uncontrollably, followed by waves of burning fever. This pattern repeated for months. I was frail, weak, convinced at times that I would not survive. Each day, I wondered if it would be my last. And yet, slowly, my body fought back. Against all odds, after many months, I began to recover. I lived, though thinner and weaker, scarred by the memory of those endless nights of fever.

But not everyone was as fortunate. I had friends whose lives were cut short before they even reached adulthood. One of them went to gather wood in the forest —a simple task we all did to cook our meals and warm our homes. The next day, he returned sick, burning with fever, and before another sunrise, he was gone. No medicine, no treatment, only helpless prayers and grief. Another friend, still a child, was playing on the grass field when a stray dog bit him. Within days, he too was dead—rabies taking his life as swiftly as the war claimed others.

Life in the village was brutal. We depended on nature for everything—food, water, wood, and shelter. But nature, too, could be merciless. The same forests that gave us firewood hid danger in the shadows. The same rain that nourished our rice could flood our fields and wash away our harvest. We lived in constant tension between gratitude and fear—thankful for each day of survival, yet haunted by how quickly it could end.

These were the saltless tears of our lives—shed without strength, without comfort, and without hope of change. Each loss felt like another stone laid upon our hearts. Yet somehow, we carried on. The will to live was all we had left, and even that felt fragile, like a candle flickering against the wind.

In those days, death felt as common as the sunrise. We no longer asked *why* tragedy struck, only *who* would be next. Life had become a daily gamble—one we never chose to play, yet could not walk away from. The laughter of children was fading, replaced by silence and weariness beyond their years.

Still, even in the midst of such sorrow, something within us refused to die. Perhaps it was the instinct to survive, or perhaps it was something deeper—a whisper from God we could not yet hear clearly, but that kept us breathing when everything around us said to give up.

The tears we shed were saltless because our bodies had grown too weary to produce more. Yet behind those tears, unseen, the human spirit continued to endure. We did not understand it then, but even in the darkest corners of our suffering, the faintest light was still burning.

We were broken, but not yet destroyed. Somewhere beyond hunger, disease, and fear, life still called to us—to rise, to hope, to remember that even ashes can give way to dawn.

10

THE NEW ORDER

SOCIALIST LAWS RESHAPE EVERYDAY
LIFE

By the early 1970s, the old order of life in the countryside had collapsed. Schools, once fragile shelters of learning, were gone. The bombings had leveled nearly every classroom in the villages, and since 1970, education for Cambodian children had been closed indefinitely. For most families, that was the end of schooling. Children stayed in the fields, planting rice, tending cattle, or running to bomb shelters when the planes came.

But for us Chinese families, a strange exception appeared. The Khmer Rouge, who allowed no Cambodian schools to reopen, mysteriously permitted underground schools for Chinese children old enough to run when danger struck. Why this privilege was granted, no one explained. Perhaps it was some hidden agreement with China, or perhaps the revolution saw the Chinese as useful tools for their cause. I was eleven years old at the time—old enough to dodge when planes came—and so I was enrolled.

The school was unlike anything I had known. Two teachers had been sent from China, and the lessons they brought were not just about language. The textbooks were filled with Maoist ideology—what they called *"the Little Red Book"* of Mao Zedong. The songs we were taught were not about family, village, or hope, but about revolution and devotion to Mao. I remember one song that declared: *"The love of parents cannot compare to the love of Mao Tse-tung."* Another proclaimed: *"The rebellious parties are nothing but paper tigers—frightening at first glance, but weak in reality."*

Before every lesson, we had to rehearse a hymn-like anthem: *"In the reddest eastward sky, the sun rises, China brings forth Mao Tse-tung."* The words were meant to fill our minds with loyalty, not to our families or to Cambodia, but to Mao and the cause of international communism. Free education, yes—but with the price of our hearts and minds.

I was not impressed. Even as a boy, I had heard stories of why many Chinese had fled their homeland: the Cultural Revolution, the purges, the hunger, the endless propaganda. My own father had left as a young man, seeking freedom from those very things. And yet here they were, finding their way back to us in Cambodia, dressed in the language of "education."

Still, I studied. My goal was not to be molded into an ideologue, but simply to learn the language. Despite the chaos of war all around, I found I was a quick learner. The school began with two classes: first grade for beginners, second grade for those with some knowledge already. I was placed in the first grade, but as I watched the older children, I longed to advance more quickly. By the end of the year, I approached my teacher and asked to skip directly into the third grade. To my surprise, they agreed. My parents did not understand the value of this—it was my own determination that drove me forward.

Yet even this strange privilege was fragile. In 1974, before the war ended, the underground school was closed without explanation. I would later understand why, as Angkar's plans for the country grew darker and more rigid. But at the time, it was simply another change we accepted—another part of life swallowed by war.

Around that same time, the Chinese who had been sent to teach and train us were suddenly recalled to China. No one told us why. One day, they were still among us, guiding lessons and sharing their skills; the next, they were gone. Later, I came to see that this too was part of Angkar's design. The Khmer Rouge no longer wanted any outside influence, not even from those who had once been their allies. It was as though they wanted to sever every tie with the world—to stand alone in their coming victory, pure and untainted by foreign presence. To us villagers, their departure was confusing and painful. It felt as if a bridge had been pulled away just as we were learning to cross it.

Meanwhile, Angkar continued to tighten its grip on the villages, though at first it was subtle. They promised rewards for loyalty, encouraging families to see themselves as part of a grand national mission. Hope lingered in many hearts—we believed, or wanted to believe, that these sacrifices were building something better.

Angkar spoke often of equality and honor. They told us that if we worked hard and proved ourselves faithful, our sacrifices would not be forgotten. When the war was over, they

said, we would share in the power and privilege of Angkar itself—living as equals among those who once belonged to the upper class. To many of us, who had known only poverty and hardship, it sounded like a dream worth striving for. Even though we did not fully understand what that promise meant, we clung to it. It was the only hope left in a world where everything else was being taken away.

The privileges given to Chinese families extended beyond schooling. China sent acupuncturists to train young Chinese adults in the healing arts, to serve their communities in place of the medicine we so badly lacked. My sister was chosen for this training, learning the trade of needles and meridians, of healing without Western drugs. To us, it seemed like a blessing. For once, we were not empty-handed; we had knowledge, skill, and a role to play.

We were also allowed to trade. Chinese families could sell goods in the market, while many Khmer villagers could not. But even this privilege was built on shaky ground. The currency being used was still from the Lon Nol regime—paper money that flowed through the countryside because there were no banks, no system of credit, no other way to trade. At the time, it worked. People used what was left, passing the bills from hand to hand as if they still had meaning.

Looking back, I see now how fragile it was. Anyone educated in finance would have known that this paper currency could not last. It was the money of a dying government, and in a country divided by war, its value was already an illusion. By 1973, the illusion ended. The markets no longer accepted money. With the stroke of Angkar's will, the currency vanished, and trade as we knew it was gone.

On the surface, these privileges gave us a fragile sense of security. We had schools when others did not. We had new skills, new opportunities, and even the favor of Angkar. To many, it seemed like proof that we were safe, that somehow the storm would pass over us.

But deep down, I sensed that nothing given by Angkar was free. Every favor carried a hidden cost. Every privilege was a leash. We did not yet know it, but beneath the surface, something was shifting. It was like living at the foot of a volcano: the ground seemed calm, but you could feel the heat building beneath, waiting for the moment to erupt.

11

DIGGING GRAVES, NOT SHELTERS

THE WAR REACHES CLOSER

EVERY NIGHT, we children sat outside, staring at the sky. We watched as streaks of light lit up the horizon and listened to the distant thunder of gunfire. The front-lines were not far—less than forty kilometers away, near the great city of Siem Reap, where the ancient temples of the Angkor Wat stood as silent witnesses. For us, the war was no longer just something whispered about on the radio. It was visible, audible, alive in the night sky.

By 1973, the most feared weapon in our part of the countryside was not the bombers, but the helicopters. Unlike the American planes that flew high and dropped their loads at night, helicopters came low, fast, and merciless. They could see their targets, and their bullets rarely missed. I remember when one of my friend's mothers was shot in the face during a raid. She

survived, but lost an eye. Her brother was not so fortunate; he was killed instantly. We never forgot the sound
of those blades chopping the air above us, a sound that
meant death could fall at any moment.

What made it even stranger was that these helicopter
strikes were not American. They came from Lon Nol's
forces. America's bombers, by then, flew mostly at
night, far from our villages. They had become almost
symbolic—loud, destructive, but no longer striking
directly at us. It was Lon Nol's helicopters that we
feared. And yet, when you listened to the radio reports
from the city, they told a different story. According to
the broadcasts, these operations had killed many Viet
Cong and Khmer Rouge soldiers. But we knew the
truth. We had seen with our own eyes who died—
mothers, uncles, neighbors.

The contradictions grew. From Angkar's side, I rarely
saw wounded soldiers in the backlines. It was as if they
disappeared. They rotated their men often, keeping the
fighters moving. At the time, I thought it was part of
their strength—discipline, organization, secrecy. But in
my heart, I also wondered: what happened to those
who were wounded? Why were they hidden? Perhaps
Angkar did not want the villagers to see their weakness.
Perhaps they did not

even try to care for them. In war, life was cheap, and it
seemed that those too broken to fight simply vanished.

The great American B-52 bombers had not yet been heard in our part of Cambodia. Their thunder rolled across the borderlands, pounding the edge of Vietnam and Cambodia, but in our village, the helicopters remained the greatest terror. Yet even as the machines of war hovered over us, another enemy was killing us silently: mosquitoes. Malaria spread through the countryside with ruthless consistency. It claimed more lives than bullets or bombs. Fever and chills swept through homes, stealing children, mothers, and fathers. For villagers, malaria was the true front line.

The distance between the frontlines and our village was less than forty kilometers. For someone living in the West today, that might be the distance you drive to your favorite restaurant—a short trip with music on the radio and the comfort of safety. But for us, it was a chasm. That short distance was the line between survival and annihilation, between watching the sky for beauty and watching it for fire. It was so close that we felt as though death breathed on us, yet so far that we could do nothing to change it.

We lived as if we had no fear, but the truth was different. Deep down, we carried the weight of knowing that our lives could end at any moment, without ever fully understanding what all this suffering was for. What purpose could there be in a world where mothers lost eyes to gunfire, where children wasted away with fever, where even the earth itself seemed scarred and broken?

And as if war and hunger were not enough, sickness struck us again and again. It spared no one—not even the animals we depended on. Every hot season, disease swept through the village like an invisible storm. Chickens fell first, struck by what we later came to know as bird flu. Then the cows began to weaken, collapsing in the fields before our helpless eyes. Their bodies lay still in the heat, and the smell of death lingered in the air.

We had no medicine, no knowledge, no help. Desperation drove people to gather and chant to their gods, pleading for healing. But to what I remember, their voices rose only to the empty sky. The diseases spread anyway, indifferent to our prayers. It felt as though even nature itself had turned against us—our crops failing, our animals dying, our children wasting away.

Looking back, I realize that the hardest part of those years was not just the danger we faced, but the silence it left inside us. We did not speak of fear; we did not cry out against injustice, because survival left no room for questions. The truth, like so many of our neighbors, was buried.

And we, the living, were left to sit in the shadows of graves—human and animal alike—waiting for a dawn we could not yet imagine.

12

WHEN ALLIES WITHDREW
VIETNAMESE EXIT

Toward the end of 1973, something shifted in the air. For years, the Viet Cong had been present in our countryside. They were the disciplined soldiers who had come with rifles and confidence, who trained the White Khmer, who ate at our tables, who seemed to know when the planes would come. At first, they were seen as protectors, even saviors. But suddenly, everything changed.

One day, I saw something I had never seen before. A crowd of villagers—men with knives, spears, sticks, and whatever weapons they could find—marched toward the nearby village where the Viet Cong were stationed. Their faces were no longer passive or fearful. They were angry, violent, ready to kill. Shouts filled the air, and in the clash that followed, I heard that some of the Viet Cong soldiers were killed.

Who organized it, I did not know. But in my heart, I suspected Angkar. They had long praised the Viet Cong as brothers in the struggle, but perhaps by then they saw that victory was close. The Lon Nol armies were weak, and the Khmer Rouge no longer needed anyone else's help. If they wanted to control Cambodia's future, they had to remove every outside hand— including the Vietnamese.

What struck me most was the restraint of the Viet Cong themselves. They could have fought back. They had the weapons, the training, and the power to kill the villagers who rose against them. But they did not. They followed their discipline, their protocol. They left quietly, humiliated and unwanted, in a place where they had once been welcomed as allies.

But the violence did not end there. Many Vietnamese immigrants—families who had lived peacefully among us for years—were also attacked and killed without reason. The rage that had been stirred up against the Viet Cong now turned upon them. It no longer mattered who was a soldier and who was a neighbor; their faces alone marked them as targets. When the Viet Cong withdrew, these Vietnamese families had no choice but to flee with them. There was no safe haven left in our villages. The air was thick with suspicion and hatred, and those who stayed behind faced certain death.

I remember standing at a distance, frozen, watching people I had known all my life lose their humanity in a single afternoon. I saw neighbors turn against neighbors, their eyes filled with something darker than fear —something closer to madness. I could not understand how the same hands that once helped build houses or share rice could now be raised to kill. I felt a deep sorrow, a confusion that weighed heavy on my young heart. The world I thought I knew—a world of simple kindness and respect—was vanishing before my eyes.

That day, I saw how deeply war and propaganda had poisoned the minds of ordinary people. These were the same villagers who once shared meals with Vietnamese soldiers, who once called them brothers. Now, stirred up by Angkar's whispers and lies, they turned violent, ready to kill without hesitation. It was as if the soil itself had been poisoned, and peace could no longer grow there.

The Vietnamese who remained in Cambodia also became targets. For years, the Khmer and the Vietnamese had lived uneasily side by side, with traders, farmers, and families trying to make a living. But now, that uneasy peace was shattered. Like us Chinese, many Vietnamese families had made Cambodia their home. Yet when the tide turned, hatred swept over them like fire. Those who could fled. Those who could not often paid with their lives.

It was a sad thing to witness. Once the Viet Cong had been heroes of the revolution, now they were cast out as enemies. Once villagers had welcomed them, now they drove them away with blood on their hands. Angkar explained it as a necessity: the Viet Cong needed to return to their own war, and Cambodia would fight its own battles with its own sons. But beneath those words, the truth was darker. This was not just about independence—it was about control. Angkar wanted no rivals, no allies, no outsiders.

When the Viet Cong withdrew, Cambodia stood alone. For villagers like us, it seemed at first like a victory—no more foreign soldiers living among us, no more outsiders shaping our fate. But in truth, it was the beginning of something far more dangerous.

Angkar now stood unchallenged. With no allies to share power and no outsiders to answer to, they had the freedom to shape the country in their own image. Isolation became their greatest weapon. Cut off from the outside world, we villagers no longer had other voices to listen to, no other stories to compare, no one else to turn to for protection.

At the time, we did not yet see the danger. We thought we were watching a new independence being born. But looking back, I know now that what we witnessed was the birth of a prison—one with no walls, only orders, suspicion, and fear. With the Vietnamese gone, the revolution no longer had enemies to fight outside. And so, they would soon turn inward, against their own people.

Looking back, I see those craters in the rice fields as symbols of the war itself: massive destruction with no clear purpose, scars in the earth left behind by decisions made far away. We, villagers, lived beside them, caught fish in them, and tried to make sense of a world where the strong wasted resources while the weak struggled simply to survive.

Angkar wasted nothing. While American planes dropped bombs without targets far away in the forest, the noise no longer startled us. What we feared most now was not the sound from the sky, but the orders from the ground. Angkar tightened its grip day by day. Commands flowed down from unknown leaders, and we were told to give as much as we could to the front lines—rice, livestock, tools, even our labor. By 1974, victory seemed almost within their grasp. We could feel it in their tone, in their impatience, in the way they no longer asked but commanded.

For the first time, their true colors began to show. The masks of protection and brotherhood slipped away, and what emerged was something harsher, colder, more consuming. Angkar was no longer just a guiding organization in the shadows—it had become the master of our breath, our time, and our future.

From the very beginning, we had been part of a grand deception. In the early days, they had spoken softly, promising unity, justice, and equality. They told us our sacrifices would build

a new Cambodia where all would share equally, where none would go hungry, where every peasant could stand shoulder to shoulder with the educated. We wanted to believe. We *needed* to believe. But it was all a scheme—a calculated illusion to win our trust until obedience no longer required consent.

Now the pretense was gone. Angkar no longer sought our approval; they demanded our surrender. Loyalty was not earned—it was enforced. Their promises of equality turned into commands of submission. Those who questioned vanished without a trace. Those who obeyed learned to do so without thought.

That was how Angkar revealed its true nature—not through a single act of betrayal, but through a slow, deliberate stripping away of freedom, faith, and will. What began as a movement for the people had become a system that devoured them. And by the time we realized the truth, it was too late.

We were no longer citizens of Cambodia. We were subjects of Angkar—living shadows in a world where even hope had to whisper.

13
VICTORY FORETOLD
REDUCING ARMIES FOR THE FINAL PUSH

By 1974, the sound of victory was everywhere. Each night, we could hear the steady tramp of foot soldiers on the road, their boots beating against the earth like a warning drum. They walked with purpose, heading toward some great mission, though none of us dared to ask where. Questions were dangerous. In those days, silence was safer than curiosity.

The new village leader had his orders, and we had ours. Young or old, strong or frail, every man was called to the forest with an axe in his hand. There, we cut trees and cleared land to build rows of identical houses, each no larger than a single-room studio— about five hundred square feet, perched on poles above the ground with thatched roofs. Hundreds of us labored together, erecting one after another, each house the same as the last. No one dared to ask who would live in these "new villages." Angkar gave orders, and we obeyed.

The old markets were closed. Trading was forbidden. Whatever possessions we had were no longer ours. Angkar declared that everything—our fields, our tools, our livestock—belonged to the revolution. In exchange, we would be given rations: food measured and distributed at their discretion. The freedom to work, to eat, to live—everything was now in their hands.

I remembered then the Chinese businessmen who had once been allowed to trade across the lines, risking their lives to bring back supplies from the enemy side. My brother was among them. They had served Angkar faithfully, even profitably, and for a time it seemed they were valued. Then one day, each of these men received a letter, delivered by courier with great ceremony. The letters invited them to a special gathering, a celebration to honor their service, a recognition of their sacrifice.

My brother received the same letter. But unlike the others, he was uninterested in honors. He chose instead to join the villagers in a different work assignment, helping to build a dam

away from home for more than a month. When the day of the "ceremony" came, the others went. My brother did not.

Angkar noticed his absence. Two soldiers came to our house to fetch him. My mother was home at the time, and she told them he was working in the fields and would not be back soon. They exchanged glances and spoke words my mother never forgot: *"Let's go back and let him live."* They left. My brother was spared by chance, or by providence.

The others were not so fortunate. None of the men who went to the ceremony ever returned. They had been killed. Recognition was nothing but a trap, an invitation to their deaths.

Later that year, I learned of another horror. One of my friends, who had been conscripted into the army, returned home in shock. He had fought hard on the front lines, survived battles, and expected at last a respite. Instead, his commanders took his weapon, telling him he had carried it long enough and deserved rest. At the camp, he discovered the truth. His comrades were disappearing at night—one after another—while fresh new recruits arrived to replace them. No one spoke of where the veterans went, but he soon realized the lie. They were not being given rest. They were being eliminated.

Angkar did not trust those who had seen too much, fought too long, or proven too independent. Fearful they might turn against them, they killed their own soldiers quietly, in the dark. My friend understood this just in time, and he escaped, hiding away before he, too, could vanish.

When he told me his story, I felt the shock of betrayal. Angkar was not just ruthless toward its enemies—it devoured its own. The men who risked their lives for the revolution, the soldiers who had shed blood on the battlefield, the businessmen who had supplied them— all of them were discarded when they were no longer useful.

That was the moment I understood: victory was not being built on courage or sacrifice. It was being built on fear, betrayal, and blood. And as Angkar's grip tightened, the hope that had once drawn villagers into the revolution turned into something else entirely—a future of suspicion, deception, and death.

This was only the beginning. The building of identical houses, the killing of trusted traders, the quiet elimination of seasoned soldiers—these were not random acts. They were rehearsals. Angkar was preparing for something far greater, something that would reshape not only our villages but the entire nation.

Soon, they would not just control the countryside. They would empty the cities themselves, uprooting millions overnight, and force all of Cambodia into their "new order." What we had seen in our villages was only a glimpse of the darkness to come.

For us villagers, hope became a fragile illusion we clung to in secret. We told ourselves that when the war ended, peace would finally return. We dreamed of reuniting with relatives in the cities, of hearing laughter again in the markets, of living without the constant hum of fear in our hearts. We whispered those wishes quietly, afraid even hope itself might be punished.

Years of war had drained us. The endless bombing, the hunger, the sickness—it all blended into a dull ache of survival. We were tired of running, tired of digging shelters, tired of losing friends and family. All we wanted was a return to the simple life we once knew—rice in the fields, rain in its season, and a place to rest without fear of gunfire or commands.

But deep down, something told us that the future would not favor us. The air felt heavier; the silence after each battle grew longer. Though we longed for peace, what waited ahead was not rest but ruin. The war that had stolen our youth was about to steal the very soul of our nation.

We did not yet know it, but the end of the war would not bring the peace we prayed for. It would open the gates to a darker victory—one foretold not by freedom, but by the triumph of Angkar's absolute control. The peace we dreamed of would never come. The nightmare was only beginning.

When the final gunfire faded and the radios shouted of victory, the countryside fell strangely silent. For the first time in years, we could hear the wind moving through the palm trees, the distant call of birds returning to the fields. Some said it was peaceful. Others said it was only the calm before something greater.

We wanted so much to believe that it was over—that the suffering had reached its end. Mothers smiled faintly through their weariness, fathers spoke of rebuilding, and children dared to laugh again. The smoke had lifted from the horizon, but not from our hearts. Beneath the relief lay an uneasiness we could not name.

Angkar's flags rose higher. The cadres' voices grew sharper. Orders replaced promises. And though the war was declared won, the faces of those who ruled us no longer spoke of freedom—they spoke of control.

In the stillness of those days, we could not yet see the roads filling with dust, the endless lines of people walking toward the unknown. We did not yet see the empty cities or the tears that would follow. But the wind had already changed. The peace we hoped for had never truly come—it had only stepped aside for a deeper darkness to begin.

PART THREE

DEATH SHADOWS

14

A COUNTRY CAPTURED

THE FALL OF PHNOM PENH

THE AIR in April 1975 was heavy, subdued, almost strange. It was not the silence of peace, nor the relief of joy, but something we could not quite name. It felt as though the land itself was holding its breath, waiting. I was fifteen years old—old enough to sense that something irreversible was happening, yet too young to fully understand its weight. And then the announcement came. The new voice on the radio declared that Phnom Penh had fallen. The Khmer Rouge had captured the capital. Cambodia, they said, was finally free. The war was over. For us villagers, it was proclaimed as a victory. Hope surged through the countryside like a rising tide. At last, the long years of bombs and fear seemed to have reached their end.

The new voice on the radio declared that Phnom Penh had fallen. The Khmer Rouge had captured the capital. Cambodia, they said, was finally free. The war was over. For us villagers, it was proclaimed as a victory. Hope surged through the countryside like a rising tide. At last, the long years of bombs and fear seemed to have reached their end.

Celebrations erupted. Villagers cheered. Soldiers fired their rifles into the air in place of fireworks. People danced, sang, and embraced one another as if a new dawn had come. We believed it was the beginning of a different Cambodia—one rooted in our culture, our traditions, our pride as a people. At that moment, no one wanted to think about what came next. Joy was too rare, too fragile, to let the future intrude.

A strange new language accompanied the victory. The radio spoke of *"old people"* and *"new people."* We were told that villagers like us—the old people—had won the war, and that the "new people" from the cities would now follow our lead. It was strange to hear. We had always thought of ourselves as one people, one nation. Now, suddenly, we were divided into two. We did not yet understand what it meant, but the words planted the first seeds of suspicion.

Still, in the moment, hope outweighed worry. I remember thinking like a child with a dream—that perhaps now I could go to the city and visit my relatives. My mother's siblings lived there, most of them wealthy, except for her older brother and herself, who had chosen the countryside. Before the war, my mother once took me and my younger brother to visit her parents. They lived with my uncle, who owned a bookstore. For me, it was like stepping into another world. Shelves filled with books I had never seen before opened my eyes to knowledge, to ideas, to the beauty of learning. That visit left a mark on me, sparking a love for study that carried me even when the world around us collapsed.

As the villagers celebrated, I clung to that dream. I imagined reuniting with family in the city of Siem Reap, walking through the bookstore again, maybe even finding my way to education and a brighter future. The city seemed so close, and with peace, perhaps it could be part of my life once more. But dreams are fragile things. What I did not know was that this celebration was built on illusion.

For those in the city, I can only imagine the feelings that day. Ordinary families must have felt relief that the war was finally over. Perhaps they too dreamed of reunion, of meeting rural relatives they had not seen since the fighting began. That would have been a natural, human hope. Yet, beneath the relief, danger was already stirring. The high-ranking officials had fled before the fall, escaping to safer lands. Those who stayed behind—soldiers, intellectuals, and ordinary citizens alike—would soon be subject to the harsh new order of Angkar.

In the villages, we cheered, believing victory meant freedom. In the cities, perhaps people dared to hope the nightmare of war was ending. But history would show that both hopes were illusions. What we thought was the dawn of peace was, in truth, the beginning of a darker night.

The consequences of that false hope came swiftly. Families who had lived in their homes for generations —homes built with the labor of fathers and grandfathers, filled with memories of births, weddings, and prayers—were suddenly told they had only three hours to leave. They could take only what they could carry. Everything else—land, house, possessions—was left behind, claimed by Angkar. Imagine the shock: to step across the threshold of your own home barefoot, knowing you would never return, driven not by choice but by command.

The separation that followed was more than physical. Husbands were divided from wives, parents from children, brothers from sisters. Entire neighborhoods were scattered across the countryside, forced into labor camps where survival itself became uncertain. The hope of reunion often ended in silence, as loved ones disappeared without a trace. The dream of peace turned to the reality of death, starvation, and lifelong grief.

Some must have thought about escape, imagining they might flee to Thailand, Vietnam, or even beyond. Yet many stayed, trusting it would be safer to remain. That decision, so natural at the time, often sealed their fate. In the past, nothing in Cambodian life had prepared anyone for this. No history or memory warned them that their own people would one day force them to abandon everything and march toward the unknown.

I try to imagine myself in their place. Having lived here in America for four decades, if I were told to leave my home within three hours, barefoot and empty-handed, I would not know what to do. I would be lost, bewildered, and broken. The trauma alone would crush me. That was the reality faced by those in Phnom Penh and across Cambodia. Their loss was not just of houses or possessions—it was the shattering of identity, family, and belonging. It was the beginning of a long night that many would not survive.

The contrast could not have been greater. The people thought the war had ended. They believed the sound of gunfire had finally been silenced, that peace had returned, and that life could slowly be rebuilt. They dared to hope for rest, for family reunions, for the chance to live again without fear.

But Angkar's plan was the opposite. Where the people dreamed of rebuilding, Angkar planned to dismantle it. Where the people longed for reunion, Angkar plotted separation. Where the people hoped for peace, Angkar prepared for war—not against foreign enemies, but against its own people.

That April day was not the end. It was the beginning. The beginning of forced evacuations, of endless marches into the countryside, of labor camps and starvation, of silence and death. The "liberation" so many celebrated became captivity. The peace so many imagined became the Killing Fields.

15

EXODUS TO NOWHERE
THE EVACUATION OF THE CITIES

FOR THE FIRST time in years, we were allowed to celebrate. When the war was over, the Khmer Rouge had captured Phnom Penh, Siem Reap, Battambang, Kompong Cham, and every other city once held by Lon Nol. Angkar gave us a brief taste of peace. For nearly two weeks, villages rejoiced, as though a new dawn had come. Laughter returned, drums beat, and people dared to hope. But beneath the surface, the air was heavy, waiting for something else to begin.

Then we saw them.

They came in waves, stretching endlessly along the dusty roads—families driven out of the cities, stripped of their homes and possessions. Old and young, mothers carrying infants, children clinging to their parents, the elderly stumbling under the weight of miles they had never walked in their lives. Their faces told the story long before their voices did: exhaustion, despair, suffering without care or compassion.

Armed soldiers marched them forward with harsh orders, treating them like criminals. Some families pushed motorbikes. Others tried to roll their cars along the road, but one by one, the vehicles broke down and were abandoned. Villagers scavenged the tires, cutting them into sandals, for shoes had become a luxury none of us could afford.

What struck me most was how few men walked with their families. On the roads, soldiers separated the males—fathers, brothers, sons—and recruited them for the "new government." They promised rewards, honor, and a role in rebuilding Cambodia. Some believed and stayed behind. Others sensed the danger and resisted. But rumors soon spread of what really happened: men and women bound together, loaded onto buses, and driven away to disappear forever.

Those who managed to stay with their families tried to survive by denying who they were. Educated men claimed to be farmers. Teachers pretended they could not read or write. Civil servants insisted they were only servants for the wealthy. Everyone knew Angkar was searching—searching for those tied to the old government, for anyone educated, for anyone who could think for themselves. They wanted a new Cambodia built only on the backs of peasants, and everyone else was marked for elimination.

And then it dawned on me. The identical houses we had been ordered to build, the strange new villages rising in the forests—these were for them. These weary, displaced families were being marched into lives they could not survive. How could city people, who had never planted rice or cut firewood, endure in places where even we villagers barely scraped by? How could mothers with small children build a future in a wilderness where there was nothing? The truth settled in my heart like a stone: these houses were not for new beginnings. They were suffering.

Some of us tried to show kindness. We gave food, whatever little we could spare, and offered water to the exhausted travelers. They ate with tears in their eyes, grateful for rice or soup they never would have touched before, food prepared without cleanliness, in villages with no wells or sanitation. It was not enough, but it was something human in a time when humanity was slipping away.

Later, we learned how sudden it had been. In Phnom Penh, in Siem Reap, in Battambang, in every city across Cambodia, families were ordered to leave their homes immediately. No warning. No preparation. Parents at work, children at school, husbands away at the market—families were torn apart in an instant, never to see each other again. Many believed it was only temporary, that they would return in a few days. They left pots simmering on stoves, clothes drying on lines, and books open on tables. But they never went back.

It was called liberation. In truth, it was an exile.

That day, as I watched the endless line of weary faces pass through our village, I realized Cambodia itself had become a prison. The people were no longer citizens; they were captives of Angkar. And all of us—city and countryside alike—were being marched, step by step, into a future of darkness.

For me, it carried another weight. Deep inside, I still held the dreams of a boy. I longed for the chance to return to school, to sit in a classroom again, to hold a book instead of a hoe. I thought perhaps, with the war over, such a door might open. I also dreamed of visiting my uncle and aunt, of laughing with my cousins in the city. I imagined the joy of reunion, the warmth of family bonds renewed after so many years apart. In my heart, it seemed possible. Perhaps they dreamed the same—that one day we would meet again in peace, not in fear.

But those dreams were never fulfilled. The very people I longed to see were themselves being torn from their homes, driven into the wilderness with nothing but what they could carry. Instead of reunion, there was separation. Instead of classrooms, there were fields of forced labor. Instead of laughter, there was silence.

No one could have predicted what was to come. We thought the war's end meant a new beginning. But it was not freedom that awaited us—it was exile, hunger, and loss. The future we imagined was stolen before it could even take shape.

Thus ended our hopes. What began as a march of return became an exodus to nowhere. We thought we were walking toward peace, but we were only walking deeper into the night.

16

ENEMIES AMONG US
ROUNDUPS, ARRESTS, AND SILENT EXECUTIONS

THIS WAS the darkest period in Cambodia's history. If you travel there today, you can visit museums where the skeletons remain, silent witnesses to the horrors that consumed our land. But in those days, it all unfolded so quickly, so suddenly, that even living through it, I could not believe it was real. There had been no great uprising, no civil upheaval among ordinary people. We had lived peacefully under the King, loyal though neglected, never imagining such cruelty could take root among us. Where did this darkness come from? How did our leaders turn against their own people?

The names we once heard on the radio—Khieu Samphan, Ieng Sary, and Son Sann—slowly faded into silence. A new name began to surface, whispered first and then spoken openly: Pol Pot. He seemed to appear out of nowhere, and yet he rose like a shadow spreading across the nation.

At the time, I wondered who he was. Did he act out of paranoia, distrusting even his closest comrades? Was it vengeance, like the old Chinese films we sometimes watched, where a wronged man plots revenge against the world? Or was it something darker, more deliberate —a plan to rebuild Cambodia by destroying it first?

Later, I would learn more. Pol Pot was not a peasant but a man of education. Born Saloth Sar in 1925 to a relatively well-off farming family, he studied in Phnom Penh and later in Paris, where he was exposed to communist ideology. In France, he absorbed radical ideas of Marxism and Maoism, and when he returned to Cambodia, he carried with him not only the theories of revolution but the desire to outdo his teachers. If Mao had remade China, Pol Pot would remake Cambodia. Only he went further: he sought to erase everything—cities, money, schools, religion, even families—until nothing was left but the peasants and the land. Unlike Hitler, who targeted the Jews as an enemy race, Pol Pot turned against his own people. He believed that to build a pure agrarian society, millions had to die.

And so, the roundups began.

Men from the cities who had been marched into the countryside were never safe. Angkar kept searching, kept rooting them out, no matter how well they tried to hide. Every village was ordered to be vigilant, to report anyone who seemed suspicious, anyone who might be "hiding their identity." The definition of an enemy shifted constantly. One day, it was former soldiers. Another day, it was teachers, doctors, or those who could read. Even wearing glasses could mark you as intellectual, and thus a threat.

Angkar encouraged villagers to betray one another. To turn someone in was to show loyalty. To accuse was to prove yourself trustworthy. Promotions were not given for skill or merit, but for the willingness to take another life for the revolution. Neighbors watched neighbors. Friends watched friends. Even families could not trust one another. Children were encouraged to spy on their parents, to report careless words, to denounce their own blood in the name of Angkar.

Isolation became the weapon. We were told to live together as one, but in truth, each of us lived alone, mistrusting those around us. It was like watching a herd of animals: the strong and united could not be caught, but the one who strayed, the one who was different, became prey. That was Pol Pot's design. He created a society of suspicion, where fear fed on fear, and where silence was the only shield.

We hardly had time to grasp what was happening. It all moved so quickly—trust crumbled, suspicion spread, and death followed close behind. We were still reeling from the war, still holding onto fragments of hope, when the ground shifted beneath our feet. In the midst of it all, we almost forgot the King. The very man whose voice had once stirred loyalty, who had called us to join him in revolution—his name vanished. We did not hear him again. No one knew what had become of him, the one we had loved and trusted.

It was as if his voice had been swallowed by the darkness he helped unleash. And in its place, there was only Angkar. The King had promised to return. Instead, what returned was terror.

This was not war anymore. This was extermination by design—a system that devoured its own people, stripping them of trust, of dignity, of life itself. The King's voice faded, and Angkar's voice became the only one left to obey.

We saw it unfold before our very eyes. The "new people," those who had come from the cities, were treated not as fellow Cambodians but as enemies—as prisoners of war in their own homeland. They were herded into the villages, their faces pale with exhaustion, their hands blistered from labor they had never known. They carried their children and what little they could salvage, but they also carried the unbearable weight of fear and humiliation.

They were given no rest, no compassion, no dignity. The cadres barked orders, stripped them of possessions, and demanded they work as though their survival depended on proving their loyalty to a cause that had already condemned them. Families were separated. Mothers wept in silence. Hunger followed them like a shadow that never lifted. Even showing kindness toward them became dangerous—an act that could mark you as a traitor. The world had turned upside down, and no one could tell the difference between guilt and innocence anymore.

I watched these things happen, powerless to stop them. I wanted to believe that someone would intervene—that reason, mercy, or humanity would return. But none did. The cruelty I witnessed was beyond words. It was as though Angkar had drained compassion from the hearts of men and replaced it with cold obedience.

Even now, I cannot fully comprehend it. How could one man—Pol Pot—allow his heart to be so consumed by hatred and evil? How could an entire nation be persuaded to turn against its own? These questions have followed me all my life, echoing through every memory of those years. There are no answers that make sense—only the ache of what was lost and the silence that remains where voices once sang.

What I know is this: we were a nation betrayed from within. Our greatest enemy was not foreign invaders, but our own blindness, our willingness to trust those who spoke of unity but delivered only death. The faces of my countrymen—once filled with hope—became faces of ghosts. And as I stood among them, I realized that the Cambodia we had known was gone, swallowed by a darkness so deep that even the dawn seemed afraid to rise.

17
EMPTY TEMPLES, HOLLOW HEARTS
THE SILENCING OF FAITH IN CAMBODIA

FOR AS LONG AS anyone could remember, Buddhism was the soul of Cambodia. The saffron-robed monks were more than teachers or priests—they were the moral compass of our people. They blessed marriages, chanted at funerals, guided children in learning, and reminded us of compassion in a world that often knew only struggle.

Every village revolved around its temple. The temple grounds were where we gathered, where festivals took place, where we celebrated New Year and **Pchum Ben**, where incense smoke curled into the sky carrying the prayers of generations. Even the poorest villager could kneel before the Buddha and feel dignity in that moment of worship. This was the tradition that had passed on through generations that I was accustomed to.

Pchum Ben, known as the Festival of the Dead, is one of Cambodia's most sacred observances. It spans fifteen days, usually in late September or early October, and is rooted in the belief that during this time the gates of the spirit world open, allowing the souls of the departed to visit the earth. Families wake before dawn to prepare offerings of rice, cakes, and food, which they bring to the pagoda to share with the monks and dedicate to their ancestors. Prayers are lifted not only for family members who have passed away but also for the forgotten souls—those with no one left to remember them.

As I remember, in the villages, people would build small rafts using banana trunks, peeling away the outer layers and binding them together. On these rafts, they placed food and candles—symbolic gifts to send the spirits back to where they came. Before sunrise, villagers would carry the rafts to the riverbank, light the small candles, and gently push them into the water. As the flickering flames floated downstream, they lit up the dark surface of the river like a trail of stars. The entire village would gather in quiet reverence, watching the lights drift away, each one carrying love, remembrance, and hope.

For us, Pchum Ben was more than a ritual. It was a moment when the living and the dead met in gratitude —a reminder that our lives were part of a greater story that stretched far beyond our years.

After the Khmer Rouge victory, that sacred order collapsed overnight.

Pol Pot decreed that monks must abandon their robes and return to civilian life. Men who had dedicated their entire existence to meditation, to humility, to prayer, were stripped of their identity in a single command. Their shaved heads and saffron robes disappeared. Some were forced into field labor, others vanished altogether. The revolution had no use for prayer, only for work.

Worship was forbidden. The sacred temples, once filled with chanting and song, now stood silent and empty. The stillness was not peaceful; it was desolation. I remember walking past a temple that had once been alive with color and sound. Now its doors hung open, its courtyard deserted, its spirit hollow. It was as though the heart of the village had stopped beating.

Worse still, the statues of the Buddha—objects of devotion that had stood for centuries—were desecrated. Faces of stone and wood that had looked upon generations with serene compassion were shattered, defaced, reduced to rubble. Where once people bowed in reverence, now only broken fragments lay in the dust. It was not just the destruction of religion—it was the deliberate humiliation of a culture.

At first, villagers whispered their grief. They longed for the sound of chanting, the comfort of ritual, the hope that prayer had always brought. But fear silenced them quickly. No one dared speak of missing the monks or mourning the statues. Angkar demanded that we see the Buddha as useless, the monks as parasites. To question was to risk suspicion, and suspicion meant death.

The absence grew heavier with time. Without the monks, there were no blessings for new babies, no chants to guide the dead, no festivals to bind the community together. The rituals that had given shape to life itself were gone. We had been stripped not only of freedom, but of meaning.

This was Pol Pot's deeper victory. By destroying the temples, he destroyed more than buildings. By scattering the monks, he scattered the spirit of a nation. By smashing the Buddha, he shattered the mirror in which Cambodians had always seen themselves.

Looking back, I realize this was not just an attack on faith. It was part of the larger design of Angkar: to erase and to tear down everything old, everything that carried memory, everything that reminded us of who we had been. Without the monks, without the Buddha, without the sacred festivals, we were left hollow. And into that emptiness, Angkar planted its own god —obedience.

Religion had always been the moral compass of Cambodia. The temple was not only a place of worship but the center of village life—where children learned respect, where the old found wisdom, where the people were reminded of right and wrong. It was woven into our festivals, our marriages, our funerals, our seasons of planting and harvest. It reminded us that there was good and evil, that every action carried consequences, and that life was sacred.

Angkar understood this. That is why they tore it away. By stripping us of religion, they stripped us of conscience. Without monks to guide, without sacred words to measure against, the people no longer had a framework to question what was happening. There was no voice to say, *"This is evil."* To criticize was to invite death. And so silence replaced truth, and fear replaced faith.

Empty temples. Hollow hearts. That was the Cambodia Pol Pot created. By erasing our faith, he unchained cruelty and ensured that the unthinkable could be carried out—not by foreign invaders, but by Cambodians against Cambodians, without resistance, without uprising. When the temples fell silent, so did the conscience of a nation.

But Pol Pot's ambition went even deeper. It was not enough for him to destroy our religion—he wanted to replace it. He wanted every heart and mind to be devoted to him alone, as if he were god himself. In his world, there was no room for heaven, no room for mercy, only his voice, his ideology, his will. He declared himself the compass of a new morality, a man who could define right and wrong without the burden of a soul.

Angkar became his altar, and obedience to his worship. To question him was blasphemy. To resist was death. Under his rule, faith was no longer placed in the divine but in a man who demanded total surrender to his cause. And with that, Cambodia was plunged into its darkest chapter—a world where morality was rewritten, love was replaced by loyalty, and compassion was branded as weakness.

This was the birth of what the world would come to know as *the Killing Fields*. A nation once rich in spirit and kindness had been turned into a graveyard of its own people. The sound of prayer was gone, replaced by the silence of fear. And in that silence, humanity itself seemed to vanish.

18

REBRANDING THE PEOPLE
NEW IDENTITIES, SEGREGATION, AND CONTROL

AFTER THE DECLARATION of liberation and the celebrations of victory faded, life settled into a new and uneasy routine. The "new people" from the cities had been sent away—where no one knew. Travel between villages was forbidden unless assigned by Angkar. We were trapped in invisible boundaries, waiting for the next command.

Even in the heaviness of those days, I still clung to hope. Somewhere deep in my heart, I wondered if this might be the moment I could study again. It was naïve, perhaps, but learning had always been my lifeline. While others spoke of survival, I dreamed of books.

Then one morning, my world collapsed. Three soldiers arrived at our door. They told my mother we had three hours to pack our belongings. Angkar had ordered us to move to a new place already prepared for us. At first, I thought it was a nightmare, but the harshness in their voices told me this was real.

We had witnessed the exodus of city people through our village. We had watched them suffer, carrying what they could, leaving everything behind. Now it was happening to us. What I had pitied from a distance was now my own fate.

Angkar announced that society had been divided into two categories: *"new people"* and *"old people."* The "old people" were those who had lived under Khmer Rouge control during the war; the "new people" were those from the cities. As ethnic Chinese, we suddenly found ourselves stripped of the privilege we once held. We were no longer trusted, no longer considered part of the community we had grown up in. Overnight, we became "new people"—outsiders, prisoners of our own land.

The humiliation cut deeply. I had lived all my life in Cambodia. I spoke Khmer, worked the fields, and shared the hardships of my neighbors. I had never thought of myself as anything but Cambodian. But now, because of my heritage, we were branded, segregated, and cast aside. My friends no longer dared to help us. Soldiers stood watching, dictating what we could take and what we could not. Even the fruit trees in our yard, which I had always taken for granted, seemed suddenly precious beyond words. I looked at them, knowing I might never taste their fruit again. That thought broke me, and I could not compose myself.

Three hours may sound like enough time to prepare, but under such fear, it felt like the clock was racing against us. My mind was torn between panic and sorrow. The one thing I knew I must take were my books—my Chinese readers, my few Cambodian texts. They were neatly stacked, treasures I had guarded because I had never given up learning. Even then, in the shadow of exile, I believed I was born to study. Looking back, I see it now as a seed planted by the Creator Himself, a purpose hidden within me even in the darkest days.

We were allowed two wagons, pulled by two cows, because my oldest brother was married and had a son. One wagon was given to him, one to our family. They were ours in name, but the truth was clear: everything we had now belonged to Angkar.

When the time came to leave, my heart broke. This was not like any journey before. It was not a visit to relatives or a trip to another village. This was exile. This was farewell to the home that had shaped me, to the neighbors I had grown up with, to the land that had always been mine in spirit if not in title. I walked away knowing we might never return.

That day, I felt fear pierce me for the first time. Not the fear of bombs, or of hunger, or of soldiers. It was the fear of betrayal—the realization that I no longer belonged to the country I had always called home. We were no longer accepted, no longer trusted, no longer free. We had been rebranded, stripped of our identity, and marched into an unknown future.

It was a sad day. Perhaps the saddest of my life.

Being forced from our home was only the beginning. We soon learned that "new people" meant more than just a different label. It meant suspicion. It meant harder labor, harsher treatment, and fewer rations. It meant being watched, doubted, and reminded every day that we were not trusted.

For Angkar, "new people" were not fellow Cambodians. We were outsiders, burdens, even enemies within. And in time, that rebranding would cost countless lives. What began with humiliation and exile would soon descend into something darker—purges, hunger, and death.

At first, I struggled to understand it. Why was I suddenly not part of the community I had known all my life? I had served beside my neighbors, suffered the same war, and endured the same bombs. Yet now, with a single word—*new people*—all of that was erased. The privileges of belonging, of being trusted, were stripped away. We were branded so that even in the smallest details, the difference could not be forgotten.

It hurt more than I can describe. To be told I was less. To be treated as though I was unworthy. To realize that my place in society had been decided for me, not by my deeds or my character, but by decree. The pain was sharp because it was not just physical—it was the tearing away of dignity.

But this was the design of Angkar. By branding us, they made the division clear. We were the "new," the unwanted, the expendable. They wanted us to wear that identity until we believed it ourselves. And they wanted the "old people" to see us as different, as lesser, so that when the purges began, there would be no hesitation. It was a system of separation, humiliation, and ultimately, elimination.

That rebranding was not just a word. It was a death sentence, waiting for its time. We were no longer people. We were only labels, waiting to be erased.

When the time came to pack our belongings, soldiers watched us closely. Their eyes followed every movement, every item placed into a bag—as though nothing we owned was truly ours anymore. They took notes, whispered among themselves, and made it clear that even the smallest possession could be confiscated at any moment. The air was heavy with suspicion. We could feel it pressing on our backs as we worked in silence.

Even our neighbors, the ones who had once shared food and laughter with us, now stood at a distance. They did not understand what was happening, but they dared not ask. Fear had taught everyone to look away. It was the new order of Angkar: obedience without question, distance without compassion.

I could not imagine what my friends must have thought as they watched us go. Perhaps pity. Perhaps relief that it was not them. But from that moment on, my family and I were marked. We could no longer associate with those we once called friends. We had lost our place, our dignity, our privilege—by Pol Pot's design.

That day, I realized that rebranding was not about names or categories. It was about control—about stripping away every trace of belonging until we accepted the lie that we were nothing. And once we believed that, they no longer needed to erase us; we had already begun to disappear inside.

19

THE NEW HOUSE

RESETTLEMENT, UNIFORMITY, AND THE DEATH OF HOME

THE JOURNEY to our new home was short. Soldiers marched us, not far from the village where I had grown up, to a place I recognized with a sickening jolt. It was the very forest Angkar had once ordered us to clear, the ground where we had built rows of identical houses months before. Later, I understood why. Those houses had not been built for strangers. They had been built for us.

When we arrived, my heart sank. There were eight people in my family. How could we all live together in one tiny single-room hut? My older brother, who was married and had a child, was given the house next door. The rest of us were crammed into one small space with a thatched roof and raised wooden floor. There was no room for questions, no room for complaints. To question Angkar was death. We had no choice but to accept what was given.

We unpacked the little we had brought. My second brother, always the calmest among us, had prepared in secret. He had hidden salt and rice under haystacks meant for the cows, away from soldiers' eyes. Those small acts of foresight were dangerous, but they kept us alive. As we laid out our few belongings, soldiers stood over us, watching carefully. When we finished unpacking, they inspected everything again, taking away more.

We were told we had too many things. In this new order, ownership was a crime. Piece by piece, they stripped us down until it felt as though nothing truly belonged to us anymore.

Then, without warning, they told us we had been given the wrong house. Everything we had just unpacked had to be packed again, carried again, moved again. The exhaustion pressed heavy on us, but fear pressed heavier. No one knew what would happen if we resisted.

As we worked, disaster struck. My second brother, the one we relied on most, stepped on a large thorn. We had no shoes, no protection, and the thorn pierced deeply into his foot. With no hospital, no medicine, no surgery, all we could do was wait. Days passed until the infection swelled, forcing the thorn to poke through the skin. Only then could it be pulled out. Until that day, he limped in silence, bearing his pain as best he could.

By the time we finished unpacking the second time, the sun had sunk, and darkness covered us. We were weary to the bone, yet the soldiers returned once more. Again, they inspected. Again, they took more. Each time they left us with less—until we had almost nothing at all.

We had brought with us two dogs, faithful companions who had been part of our lives for years. That night, as I looked at them, my heart ached. I worried not only for us, but for them. How could we feed them when we barely had enough for ourselves? Even in the shadow of fear, hunger, and exhaustion, I felt the sting of help-lessness for my beloved animals.

That day, the meaning of "home" changed forever. What Angkar gave us was not a home. It was a house —small, uniform, stripped of comfort, stripped of free-dom, stripped of dignity. It was not a place to belong, but a place to be watched. A place to be controlled. A place to remind us that nothing, not even our lives, was truly our own.

Home had always meant belonging. It was the place where families gathered around food, where neighbors came to visit, where fruit trees shaded our yard, and where the laughter of children made even the poorest house feel rich. A home was not only walls and a roof —it was roots, memory, safety, and love.

But under Angkar, "home" became something else. It was no longer a place of belonging, but a tool of control. The identical houses erased individuality. The inspections stripped us of dignity. The rules silenced our voices. Even the smallest comfort, like feeding our dogs or hiding a little salt, became an act of defiance.

It was then that I began to understand what Angkar had promised during the war—that the poor would reign and the rich would pay. On the surface, the identical houses looked like the fulfillment of that promise. No one owned more than another. No house was larger, no family appeared richer. In this new order, Angkar declared, there would be equality—no rich, no poor, only one class of people.

But it was an illusion. These houses were not symbols of fairness, but of erasure. They were built to remind us that we had no freedom—not even the freedom to shape our own lives. Our identities were flattened, our differences erased, our rights stripped away. The sameness of the houses was not equality—it was control.

In the new house, we did not live as a family—we lived as prisoners. What had once been a sanctuary was turned into a cage. And that day I realized, perhaps for the first time, that Angkar's greatest weapon was not only death, but the slow destruction of what it meant to be human.

The houses looked identical, but they were not homes. They were monuments to our loss—proof that in Angkar's Cambodia, we belonged not to ourselves, but to the regime. In Angkar's houses, we were equal only in our captivity.

I had never imagined that Angkar could become such an instrument of evil—so devoid of conscience, compassion, or reason. What was once a movement that promised justice had turned into a machinery of cruelty. We, the Chinese descendants, were treated as though we had committed a crime simply by existing. Our heritage, once a source of pride, became a mark of shame.

In truth, our families had sacrificed much to support Cambodia's struggle and growth. We had worked the land, traded goods, paid our dues, and stood beside our neighbors. Yet none of that mattered to Angkar. They cared nothing for our loyalty or our labor. We were not judged by merit, but by blood. Our ethnicity defined our fate.

That was the day I understood that in Angkar's Cambodia, justice was not blind—it was brutal. The new houses stood as a silent testimony to that truth: identical walls built to erase identity, and a uniform life designed to break the human spirit.

The new village where we were placed—designated for us as the "new people"—was not far from my old home. It was only about three miles away, yet it felt like a world apart. Between those few miles stretched an invisible chasm that no one dared to cross. We were forbidden to visit our old friends or even to speak with those who once shared our laughter and labor. The familiar paths that once led us home were now closed, guarded by fear and suspicion.

From our new settlement, I could still see the outline of my old village in the distance—the same fields, the same trees—but it no longer belonged to me. It was so close, yet so far. We had been stripped of our place, our voice, and our privilege. The road that once led to friendship and belonging had become a road of exile. What had once been home was now only a memory, unreachable and fading.

Every morning, the sound of the gong pulled us from sleep before dawn. We rose not as free people but as subjects of Angkar's command. The routine was relentless—work, silence, obedience. Even the air seemed to belong to them.

Neighbors who once shared laughter now spoke in whispers. Families feared one another, never knowing who might be listening. The smallest gesture—an extra grain of rice, a kind word, a moment of rest—could be seen as rebellion. We lived in constant fear that a single mistake might cost us our lives.

In those days, I began to understand that Angkar's war was not just against bodies—it was against the soul of a nation.

20

THE PURGE BEGINS
FEAR AS THE NEW LAW OF THE LAND

THE MORNING after we moved into the new house, the illusion of normal life vanished. Before the sun rose high, the entire village was ordered to gather in the open field. Soldiers stood watch as the new leader barked instructions—his voice cold and final. Confusion rippled through the crowd. We were told where to stand, what to say, how to behave, and, most painfully, how to live from now on.

That morning marked the first time in my life that my family had to wait for someone else to give us food. The rations were meager, yet we dared not complain. Hunger was no longer just a condition—it was a command. What we ate, where we worked, even when we could breathe freely, all depended on Angkar. Everyone was assigned a role. My mother and siblings were sent to different work groups, each under strict supervision. As for me, I was told to care for the animals—at least for the moment. The cows still needed to graze, though I knew even they no longer belonged to us. Every creature, every tool, every grain of rice was now property of Angkar.

Later that day, as I led the cows toward the fields, a heavy truth settled in my heart: freedom had not only been taken—it had been redefined. Under Angkar, to live was to obey. But nothing could prepare me for what I saw next.

Pushing through the brush in search of grazing land, I noticed a hollow in the earth—at first, I thought it was an old bomb crater. But when I looked closer, I froze. Inside the pit lay bodies—piled, unburied, discarded as though they were nothing. Men, women, even children. The smell of death hung thick in the air, and my whole body trembled. I wanted to scream, but no sound came out. Somehow, I gathered the cows and led them away as quickly as I could, my heart pounding like a drum.

When I returned home, I told my family what I had seen. Their faces turned pale. Quietly, they told me that a family from the village had gone missing. No one dared to ask questions. No one dared to speak. We all knew what it meant: if Angkar decided you did not belong, your life could be erased overnight.

That day, I understood the new law of the land—fear. It ruled more powerfully than any weapon. And from that moment on, I knew that survival would mean silence.

Soon after, a new leader was installed over us. He was not from our village but brought in from elsewhere. He was tall, fierce-looking, and carried himself with an air of authority. But he could not read or write. Someone from the Chinese community, trying to gain his favor, gave him a watch. He wore it proudly on his wrist, but he could not tell the time. When he held meetings, he shouted slogans and repeated the same phrases again and again, using big words that I doubted he even understood. Yet this man held the power of life and death over us. This was the kind of leader Pol Pot envisioned for the new society.

Food became scarcer each day. Rations were given, but never enough. Hunger gnawed at us constantly. The saddest day came when our two dogs, faithful companions through so many years, starved to death. We had no food for ourselves, let alone for them. Their absence was another wound, another reminder that everything we loved was being stripped away.

My siblings were resourceful, always looking for ways to find food. But Angkar forbade us from doing anything not directly ordered. Even gathering fruit or fishing without permission could mean punishment—

or death. We lived under constant surveillance, our every move watched.

The air itself seemed to echo with threats. From morning to night, loudspeakers blared across the village. The same phrases repeated again and again:

"The weak branch will be cut off."

"If you resist, you will be destroyed."

"If you disobey, you will lose your arm."

The words drummed into our ears until they became part of our thoughts, shaping our fear, controlling our actions. Fear was no longer just an emotion—it was the law of the land.

This was the purge. It did not arrive with warnings or announcements. It came in silence, in the night, in the disappearance of families, in the hollows filled with bodies. It came in the form of leaders who knew nothing but power, in the starvation of even our animals, in the relentless voice of Angkar echoing from every speaker.

No one could have imagined how complete the system was—designed to strip away life's purpose and dignity. Angkar's vision was not simply political; it was agricultural. A society remade into nothing but fields and labor, where education, art, religion, and even human worth were declared useless. If a person could not work the land, if they did not fit the narrow mold of Angkar's design, they were considered expendable— and then erased.

The world had already witnessed horror in the Holocaust, where Hitler's hatred singled out the Jews for destruction. But Cambodia's horror was different. Here, the killers and the victims spoke the same language, shared the same blood. Our own people turned against us, consumed by a system that demanded loyalty at the cost of humanity.

The purge was not just about eliminating the weak—it was about erasing identity, silencing conscience, and destroying anyone who carried the memory of the old world. What had been unimaginable became normal. What had been unthinkable became expected.

And from that darkness, there was no escape. For Cambodia, the Holocaust had come again—not from an enemy abroad, but from the hands of its own children. The world had once said, "Never again." Yet in Cambodia, it was happening again.

This was what it meant to *tear down the old and create the new.*

Angkar's revolution did not build a nation—it buried one. In their quest to forge a perfect society, they destroyed the very soul of our people. Families were shattered, faith was silenced, and love itself became a crime. The "new Cambodia" they created was not a land of equality, but a graveyard of humanity.

By then, fear had become part of our breathing. Every glance, every word, every silence carried risk. The village moved like a body without a heartbeat—alive, but only barely. We learned to lower our eyes, to speak less, to feel nothing. Kindness became dangerous, and trust became a memory. Under Angkar, survival meant forgetting who you were and pretending to believe in the world they were trying to create.

21

ALL BELONGS TO ANGKAR

POL POT'S DREAM, THE PEOPLE'S NIGHTMARE

ONCE WE HAD SETTLED in our new place, it became clear that nothing truly belonged to us anymore. Travel outside the village was forbidden unless Angkar gave permission. Even the wagons and cows that had carried us to this place were no longer ours. Angkar ordered us to turn them in, declaring that they now belonged to the collective. They assigned caretakers for the animals, stripping families of even the smallest sense of independence.

Soon, every part of life was reorganized. People were divided into groups by age and ability. From children barely eight years old to the elderly, everyone was assigned a unit. Families were broken apart. Parents no longer had their children at home; siblings were scattered. It was the first time I left my family, the first time I realized that home was no longer ours.

Before I left, I hid my books in the ceiling, tucking them into the thatched roof where I hoped no one would find them. Books were dangerous, but for me, they were life itself. Each year, Angkar granted us a single week to visit home. In that week, I would stay inside the house, reading my hidden books until the day came when I had to leave again. It was my secret rebellion, my way of holding onto a part of myself that Angkar could not touch.

But Angkar did not only take away homes and possessions—they claimed the children. From then on, children no longer belonged to their parents. They belonged to Angkar. The young were taught that loyalty to the revolution was greater than loyalty to family. If parents spoke words of doubt, if they whispered of longing for the old days, children were told to report them. And many did.

I knew firsthand of parents who were killed because their own children had repeated something they had overheard. Sometimes it came from anger. Husbands and wives, in the heat of argument, would let slip the truth of who they had been or what they believed. An innocent child, thinking they were doing the right thing, repeated those words to Angkar. Soon after, the parents disappeared.

It was perhaps the cruelest wound of all. Trust within families, the most sacred bond in our culture, was shattered. Parents no longer dared to speak freely in front of their children. Words of love were guarded, and silences stretched long. Children, robbed of innocence, were turned into spies. Mothers and fathers, stripped of authority, became prisoners in their own homes.

This was Pol Pot's dream: a society where nothing and no one was private, where every possession, every relationship, every life belonged to Angkar. For us, it was not a dream at all. It was the nightmare that swallowed our families, our trust, our very humanity.

When Angkar declared that *"all belongs to the collective"*, it sounded like an idea of fairness, even justice. No one would be rich, no one would be poor. Everything— land, tools, animals, wagons, even children—belonged to the State. On the surface, it promised freedom from responsibility. We were told we no longer needed to worry about food, shelter, or work. Angkar would take care of it all.

At first, it almost sounded comforting. For centuries, life in the villages had been a struggle. Families worked the same fields year after year, scraping enough rice to survive. Now, Pol Pot's voice through Angkar said, *"You will not labor for yourself. You will labor for the people."* We were told it was a new beginning, that this was true equality.

But soon the cracks appeared. Could you imagine anyone caring for your belongings the way you care for them yourself? A farmer's field, once tilled with pride, became just another piece of land. A cow, once treated like part of the family, became just another number in Angkar's ledger. A house, once filled with memories, became a unit for control.

When everything belongs to everyone, it belongs to no one. No one repairs the broken tool because it is not theirs. No one guards the crops from pests because there is no reward in the harvest. No one preserves the land because it is not their family's heritage anymore— it is simply Angkar's.

The dream of "collective care" quickly rotted into neglect, waste, and abuse. By the time people realized that no government—especially one built on fear— could nurture life the way families and individuals once did, it was too late. The system was in place. Obedience was enforced by terror.

For us villagers, there was no escape. We had no choice but to obey. To complain was to invite death. To resist was to risk not only our own lives, but the lives of our families. So we bowed our heads and carried on, even as everything we had built for generations slipped away.

The irony was bitter: they said they freed us from worry, but instead, they took away the very dignity of caring for what was ours. They stripped away responsibility, and with it, the joy of ownership, the meaning of work, and the bond between effort and reward.

Pol Pot imagined a society where loyalty to Angkar replaced love of family, where collective labor replaced individual pride, and where personal ambition was buried in obedience. But what he created was a nightmare: a society where no one truly cared, because caring had been outlawed.

For us, the lesson came at a terrible price. By giving up responsibility, we lost freedom. By surrendering ownership, we surrendered dignity. And by trusting the promise of a perfect collective, we allowed ourselves to become slaves in our own homeland.

Yet ownership was never meant to be stripped away, for it is a gift from God to all mankind. From the beginning, the Creator entrusted humanity with responsibility over what was theirs—land, labor, family, and the fruit of their hands. No one can steward or improve what belongs to them better than the one who owns it. Ownership fuels accountability, creativity, and diligence.

When the Khmer Rouge imposed the law that everything belonged to the Angkar, the result was not unity but collapse. The quality of society deteriorated because responsibility was severed from reward. There was no motivation to work harder, to plant more, to build better, or to dream bigger. When ownership was stolen, the heart of the people was crushed. And with that, chaos and despair spread like wildfire.

This truth is echoed in Scripture. In the Garden of Eden, God gave Adam the responsibility to "work it and keep it" (Genesis 2:15). Stewardship was not a burden—it was part of mankind's dignity and purpose. Likewise, Jesus' parable of the talents reminds us that God expects each person to take ownership of what He has entrusted, to multiply it faithfully, and to give an account (Matthew 25:14–30). When responsibility is removed, fruitfulness withers. When ownership is denied, the God-given drive to labor and create is quenched.

The nightmare of the Khmer Rouge proved that no system can outdo God's design. A society that erases ownership erases hope. But a people who honor God's gift of stewardship will flourish, even in hardship. True freedom comes not from control, but from responsibility under God.

22

CHILDREN OF ANGKAR
TRAINED TO HATE, TAUGHT TO KILL

IF THE SOUL of Cambodia had once been nurtured by monks and teachers, under Pol Pot, it was remade by Angkar in the image of children. The revolution did not trust the wisdom of elders, the guidance of parents, or the traditions of faith. Instead, it turned to the young—malleable, rootless, and hungry for belonging—and made them its weapon.

Most of these children came from the *old people*, the peasants who had lived under Khmer Rouge control before the war ended. They were chosen for three reasons. First, they were poor, and poverty made them dependent on Angkar for food, clothes, and purpose. Second, they were illiterate. Since schools had been closed in 1970, they had never been educated; they could not question, could not compare, could not think beyond the slogans they were taught. Third, they had grown up in war. Violence was normal to them. The sound of gunfire and the sight of death had shaped their childhood. For Angkar, these were the perfect recruits—children who could be trained to hate, to kill without hesitation, to obey without question.

The children of the *new people* were not trusted in the same way. Angkar never forgot that they came from the cities, that their parents had lived under Lon Nol. Instead of giving them weapons, they indoctrinated them differently. They were trained to listen, to watch, and to report. If a parent whispered of longing for the past, if a sibling questioned the fairness of Angkar, even if a careless word slipped out during an argument, the child was expected to repeat it. Many did. And parents were taken away because of the very sons and daughters they had once carried in their arms.

The children selected for combat training were given guns—not pistols, which were reserved for high-ranking leaders as symbols of authority—but rifles. Some of the boys were so small that the barrels of their weapons nearly touched the ground as they walked. Yet in their hands, those oversized guns were more terrifying than anything else we faced.

We feared them more than we feared the adult soldiers. Adult soldiers had power, yes, and they could kill—but sometimes we sensed a sliver of humanity in them, a hesitation, a moment of recognition that we were human too. With the child soldiers, there was nothing of that. They had been stripped of innocence and filled with hate, trained to see us not as people but as enemies, obstacles, or prey.

They could take a life for any reason—or for no reason at all. If a boy soldier disliked the way you looked, the way you walked, the way you worked, he had the authority to kill you right there in front of everyone. And many did. Public killings became lessons: *this is what happens if you displease Angkar.*

Whenever we saw them, fear pierced us to the core. We tried to act normal, careful with every word, every movement, every breath. But inside, our hearts pounded with terror. To be killed by an adult soldier was a risk of war; to be killed by a child was a nightmare without reason.

This was the society Angkar created: children carrying guns bigger than themselves, holding the power of life and death, while families, neighbors, and entire villages trembled before them. Pol Pot's dream of purity and strength had turned children into executioners—and for the rest of us, into the most terrifying face of the revolution.

Could you imagine what kind of future this would bring? A society where children were taught not to learn, but to kill. A nation where the young, instead of being nurtured, were turned into weapons against their own people. What future could such a country have?

In most nations, children represent hope—the promise of something better, a chance to build on the past and improve life for the next generation. But under Angkar, the future was built not on knowledge, compassion, or progress, but on fear, hatred, and death. Instead of preparing children to heal the wounds of war, they trained them to reopen them again and again.

This was not a revolution for a better life. It was not a new beginning. It was a purge, endless and merciless, that sought not to build but to destroy. By turning children into executioners, Angkar ensured that the future of Cambodia would not be fields of growth or homes of peace, but ruins—scattered bones, broken families, hollow villages, and empty hearts.

For every parent, this was a nightmare with no escape. To see the child they had fed, bathed, and prayed for now reporting their every word to Angkar—it was a wound deeper than hunger, deeper than fear. Many parents learned to keep silent even in their own homes, knowing that one careless word could mean death if repeated by innocent lips.

But the wound was not just Cambodia's—it was universal. For every parent in every nation, children are the most precious gift entrusted by God. They are the living hope of tomorrow, the heartbeat of every home, the reason mothers endure hardship and fathers labor without rest. To watch children stolen, not by distance or disease, but by indoctrination, is a grief beyond words.

No father should hear his child call another master. No mother should see her child taught to hate instead of love. When the innocence of childhood is replaced with chants of violence, the very image of God in a child is marred. And when a society dares to sever the sacred bond between parent and child, that society is already on the path to ruin.

The children of Angkar were not simply taught to kill —they were taught to forget who they were, whose they were, and to whom they truly belonged. That is why the memory of this tragedy is more than history— it is a warning. A warning to every generation that if we surrender the hearts of our children, we surrender the future of our world. No nation can survive when its children are no longer free to be children.

23
THE ILLITERATE RULE
INTELLECTUALS FORBIDDEN, PEASANTS EXALTED

POL POT'S new society was built on a single principle: ignorance was strength. The regime had no use for education, knowledge, or critical thought. Intellectuals, teachers, doctors, engineers—anyone who had studied, anyone who could think independently—were considered enemies. They were executed or worked to death.

In their place, Angkar exalted the illiterate. Men and women who could not read or write were considered "pure." They were easy to mold, easy to command, and easy to convince that blind loyalty was the highest virtue. They became the new leaders, chosen not for wisdom or skill but for their willingness to obey orders without question.

To be chosen by Angkar, one needed two qualities above all: the ability to endure backbreaking labor without complaint, and the heartlessness to carry out executions. Those who turned in "bad elements"—the complainers, the weak, the sick, or the ones who dared to question—were rewarded. In this way, the new society fed on betrayal, raising up leaders who thrived on suspicion and cruelty.

But the cruelty had no limits, even for those in power. After a time, many of these illiterate leaders themselves were eliminated. Pol Pot trusted no one—not his subordinates, not his comrades, not even those who had proven themselves by shedding blood. Leaders who once enforced the law with violence were suddenly accused, arrested, and executed. Their replacements learned quickly: no one was safe, not even them.

I remember hearing whispers of uprisings—places where leaders had grown too brutal, too greedy, too reckless. Ordinary people rose up in fury. Some leaders ran into hiding, only to be hunted down. Others were killed outright before Angkar sent soldiers to restore control and arrest many of the rebels.

These cracks in the system gave us, the "new people," small, fragile hope. When leaders realized that they too could be eliminated, some became more cautious, even lenient. In certain villages, rations were shared more fairly. People were treated with a little more dignity. In other places, however, the cruelty continued unchecked, and families starved. Under Pol Pot, survival often depended not on hard work alone, but on the temperament of the leader placed over you.

I was not fortunate. My village did not have one of the merciful ones. Hunger and fear pressed down on us daily. And yet, even in the cruelty, we saw the truth: Angkar's dream of a perfect society was devouring itself. Leaders killed their people, and then leaders were killed in turn. No one escaped suspicion. No one was safe.

In most nations, education is seen as the foundation of progress. Teachers shape young minds, doctors heal the sick, engineers build roads and bridges, and leaders plan for the future. Knowledge is not a threat—it is the very tool by which a country grows strong.

But in Pol Pot's Cambodia, knowledge was death. To be educated was to be distrusted. To question was to be condemned. To show wisdom was to invite suspicion. And so, the very people who could have rebuilt the country—scholars, doctors, engineers, thinkers—were silenced forever.

Angkar exalted ignorance and punished intelligence. They raised leaders who could not read a book or tell the time on a watch. And yet even these leaders were not safe. They, too, were eliminated when suspicion turned against them.

How could a government hope to build a nation if no one was safe to serve? If every leader feared his own execution, if every villager feared the gaze of his neighbor, if every family feared the voice of their own children? This was not governance. This was not a vision. It was a machine of destruction, feeding on itself until nothing remained but ruins and bones.

Among the many lives I saw broken under Angkar, two brothers remain etched in my memory. Both had been medical students in the city before the war ended—bright, educated, full of promise. They had studied to heal, to save lives, to bring hope. After the Khmer Rouge victory, they hid their identity well. They worked beside me in the fields, silent, careful, blending into the life of peasants. For a while, it seemed they might escape suspicion.

But one day, the younger brother made a mistake—an innocent one. In the countryside, people liked to pass the time with riddles, clever little puzzles of words. That day, he solved them all—one after another, effortlessly. His brilliance, which should have been admired, instead marked him for death. The village leader grew suspicious. *No ordinary farmer could think like this.*

By evening, the younger brother was arrested. He never returned. His life was ended not for rebellion, not for crime, but simply for being intelligent.

The older brother was shaken to the core. From that day on, he kept silent. He worked, he endured, but he never revealed himself again. He survived by burying his voice, by hiding his mind. And as far as I know, he still lives today in Cambodia—alive, but carrying the heavy weight of what was lost.

This was the madness of Angkar's rule. In most nations, a person's mind is his gift to his people. Doctors heal, teachers guide, leaders plan, inventors build. But in Cambodia, under Pol Pot, a person's mind was his curse. Intelligence was a death sentence. Wit could betray you. Knowledge could condemn you.

The Khmer Rouge exalted the illiterate not because they were wise, but because they were pliable. They silenced the educated not because they were dangerous rebels, but because they could think. And so, a nation that might have been rebuilt by doctors, engineers, and teachers was instead bled dry, its brightest lights extinguished.

How can a government build a country when it kills those who could serve it? How can a future stand when its foundations are destroyed? In the end, Angkar did not create a new society—it created a wasteland, a country that devoured its own children and left only silence where wisdom should have been.

And with intellect silenced, Cambodia was reduced to one vision: the land. For Angkar, books and schools were worthless. The only future they recognized was in the fields, in the backbreaking labor of rice farming. The mind was condemned, but the body was enslaved. What remained was a society where agriculture was the only engine, and survival was measured in harvests that never seemed to feed the people.

When Pol Pot seized power, the first to be targeted were the intellectuals—the teachers, doctors, engineers, students, and anyone who carried knowledge that might question Angkar's authority. Most were executed. The few who managed to survive did so by hiding their true identity, silencing their education, and pretending to be simple farmers. To admit you could read or write was to sign your own death sentence.

What remained in Cambodia was a workforce stripped of skill, stripped of wisdom, stripped of freedom to think. Every citizen was driven into the fields, but no one dared to suggest a better way or point out mistakes. To speak was to risk death. And so people bent their backs, planted rice in fear, and carried out orders they knew would fail.

Year after year, the harvests grew smaller. Canals dug in rigid straight lines ignored the land's natural slopes. Fields flooded or dried out. Crops rotted before they could be harvested. Under King Sihanouk, Cambodia had once produced abundant rice, enough to export. Under Pol Pot, the nation starved.

The tragedy was not just in the broken bodies of labor-ers, but in the silenced minds of those who could have helped. Knowledge was treated as poison. The very people who could have guided the nation were already dead, or living like shadows, too terrified to speak.

Even before the war, as a small boy, I had noticed this tension between tradition and progress. In my village, men often spent whole days hunting in the forest. Sometimes they came back with game, but often they returned empty-handed, exhausted and discouraged. If only they had been taught how to raise chickens, or pigs, or other animals, their labor would have fed the whole family and built a better future. But no one taught us to think that way. Each generation simply followed the one before, bound to customs rather than imagination. Tradition was not always wrong, but without education it became a chain—holding us in place instead of helping us rise.

And this was exactly what Pol Pot's Cambodia became: a land chained to ignorance. Muscles can dig, but only minds can design. Sweat can water the ground, but only knowledge can make it fruitful. By exalting the illiterate and condemning the educated, Pol Pot planted the seeds of his own destruction.

Looking back, I see now: the Khmer Rouge did not only kill people. They killed the nation's future. Education is not the enemy of the people—it is their greatest hope. And when a regime silences learning, it condemns itself to failure.

24
AGRICULTURE AS THE ONLY ENGINE
FARMING AS SURVIVAL, FARMING AS CONTROL

WITH INTELLECT SILENCED and trust destroyed, Angkar turned to its one obsession: the land. In their vision, books, schools, and professions were useless. Only farming mattered. Agriculture was declared the single engine of the new Cambodia.

For us, this meant endless labor. From sunrise to sunset, every man, woman, and child was sent to the fields. We dug canals, built dikes, and planted rice under the blazing sun. There was no rest except when our bodies gave out. Angkar promised that this sacrifice would create "a golden harvest," that rice would overflow and feed the nation. But the truth was different. The rice we grew did not fill our bowls. Much of it was sent away, stored, or hidden, while our stomachs remained empty.

The labor itself was merciless. Men were forced to plow fields without oxen, pulling wooden plows through mud like animals. Women carried heavy loads until their bodies bent under the weight. Children transplanted seedlings with bleeding hands, their small feet sinking in the flooded paddies. Even the elderly were not spared; they worked until they collapsed.

The quotas were impossible. Angkar demanded three tons of rice per hectare, though everyone knew such numbers could never be reached. If the harvest fell short, it was not the fault of the soil or the weather—it was blamed on the people. Failure to meet the target meant suspicion, punishment, sometimes even execution.

Among those who suffered most were the children. My younger brother Andrew was only about eleven years old when he was taken to a children's work camp. The tasks were far too heavy for his small frame—hauling dirt, carrying water, and laboring from dawn until nightfall. One day, exhausted and terrified, he tried to run away and find his way home. But he was caught.

As punishment, the cadres tied him to a tree overnight, threatening to kill him at dawn. They told him that in the morning, he would dig his own grave. He was only a child, but that night broke something deep within him. Though they spared his life, they shattered his spirit. He survived, but the boy who returned was no longer the same.

Years later, after we escaped to freedom, Andrew told me this story for the first time. I could see in his eyes that part of that frightened boy still lived inside him. He never had the chance to study under Angkar—he could not read or write when he arrived in America at fifteen. But God had other plans. The same Andrew who once could not hold a pencil went on to finish high school, earn a degree, and graduate with a master's in electrical engineering and computer science from Oregon State University. His journey is living proof that even the most broken lives can be restored.

Andrew's life became a quiet testimony that the human spirit, though crushed, can rise again. What Angkar sought to destroy—his mind, his hope, his purpose— was later restored through grace, perseverance, and opportunity. He carried the scars of that night tied to the tree, yet he also carried something stronger: the determination to live a life that proved evil could not have the final word.

When I think of those years of toil and terror, I see his face among the many who labored in the fields, believing there was no tomorrow. Yet God, in His mercy, gave us one. Andrew's story reminds me that survival alone was not the victory—it was the faith to believe that even after devastation, life could begin again.

During the dry season, we were forced to build dikes to hold water for the planting season. But instead of following the wisdom of villagers who had worked the land for generations, Angkar imposed their own "scientific" ideas. Under King Sihanouk's reign, farmers had harvested abundant crops by carefully designing smaller dikes that followed the natural slope of the land, making sure water flowed evenly to every paddy. It was practical, it was proven, and it worked.

Pol Pot rejected all of that. He and his inexperienced commanders ordered us to build massive canals in straight lines from one village to another, no matter the shape of the land. Hills and slopes were ignored. Entire hectares—about four acres each—were boxed in by dikes and connected, without regard for water levels or soil. It was backbreaking work, and in the end, the system failed. The water was uneven, the fields dried out or drowned, and crops withered.

At harvest time, Angkar treated us like bears fattened for hibernation. For a brief season, food was given generously, and we ate as much as we could, knowing it would not last. For many, it was the first time in months that they could eat freely without counting each grain of rice. Yet even that moment of abundance carried danger. I heard stories of people who died after overeating—so starved for so long that when they filled their stomachs too quickly, the rice swelled inside them, restricting their breath until they suffocated. At first, I thought these were just rumors, something told to frighten us into moderation.

But during one of those first harvest meals, I learned the truth. I was so hungry, my body so starved, that I ate without restraint. Moments later, I could hardly breathe. A sharp pressure rose in my chest, and panic set in as I remembered the stories I had dismissed. I forced myself to stop eating and stayed still, praying silently for relief. Gradually, my breathing steadied, and I survived. It was a terrifying lesson—that even in plenty, death was never far away. Under Angkar, we could die not only from hunger, but from eating.

The work in the cold season was brutal. We were ordered into the flooded fields to replant rice, standing bent over in icy water from dawn until dark. Angkar gave us only two sets of black clothing—long-sleeved shirts and trousers—that had to last us through everything. By evening, our bodies were numb, our feet swollen, the skin between our toes eaten raw by fungus. We lit fires at night just to dry our feet, and we rotated into whatever set of clothes was least wet. But when morning came, we had no choice but to put the damp ones back on and march again into the water.

As if hunger, cold, and exhaustion were not enough, Angkar placed the little soldiers—the child soldiers—over us as overseers. They patrolled the dikes with rifles hanging at their sides, watching every movement we made. Planting rice was done entirely by hand. Some men were assigned to plow the fields so the dirt beneath the water would be loosened, and the rest of us lined up in rows, working backward to transplant the rice without stepping on what had already been planted.

But the system was flawed. Sometimes the plowers missed patches of ground because the water hid the soil beneath. When that happened, seedlings floated instead of taking root. If a child soldier saw floating rice, he accused the worker of sabotage. It did not matter that it was an accident—the punishment could be death.

We learned to survive by watching each other's backs. If we saw rice floating, we quickly pressed it back into the soil before a soldier noticed. Every stalk became a matter of life and death. Could you imagine the cruelty? Just planting rice, the act that should have been life-giving, put our lives on the line every day.

I did not think too much about tomorrow, because tomorrow was never promised. We lived one day at a time, never sure if we would still be alive when the sun set again.

This was more than farming. It was controlled. By keeping us exhausted, hungry, and afraid, Angkar ensured we had no strength to resist. Our bodies were chained to the fields as surely as if we had been bound in shackles.

I seldom saw my siblings in those days. Each of us was sent to different work groups, scattered across the land. Families no longer gathered at night to share a meal; instead, we were reduced to labor units, bound not by love but by quotas. Silence grew between us. Even if we had the chance to meet, what could we say? Every word might be overheard. Every conversation might cost us our lives.

And so the land became both our lifeline and our prison. The fields that once brought joy during harvest season became places of sorrow and death. Farming was not only survival—it was submission. Angkar had destroyed education, silenced thought, broken families, and emptied temples. Now it sought to remake us into nothing but bodies working in the mud, nameless, faceless, all serving the same impossible dream.

In the end, agriculture under Pol Pot was not an engine of prosperity. It was an engine of destruction, grinding down the people until nothing remained but exhaustion, hunger, and fear.

Cambodia was once a land of plenty. Our soil was rich, our rivers full, our seasons faithful. Under King

Sihanouk, farmers harvested enough rice to feed their families and share with neighbors. The land provided life, and the people thrived with hope.

But under Pol Pot, the same fields became graveyards of the living. Angkar's hand turned abundance into famine, labor into punishment, and harvest into hunger. The fertile land that had once fed us now drained our strength, demanding more than we could give and offering nothing in return.

The true tragedy was not that Cambodia lacked resources—it was that its leaders wasted them. They destroyed the wisdom of generations, silenced the voices of knowledge, and replaced cooperation with fear. They had fields of green, but hearts of stone.

In the end, the land itself seemed to mourn. The paddies that once echoed with laughter during harvest were silent, broken only by the cries of the hungry and the slogans blaring from loudspeakers. Cambodia was still fertile, but its spirit had been made barren.

25
DIAMONDS FOR A BOWL
OF RICE
WHEN HUNGER BECAME THE CURRENCY
OF LIFE

FOR THE "NEW PEOPLE," survival was not measured in years or even months—it was measured in bowls of rice. Every day was a struggle against hunger so deep that it hollowed the body and broke the spirit. The city families, once surrounded by comforts— electricity, markets, even small luxuries—were now reduced to desperation. They had never known this kind of life. Truth be told, no one in America today could survive it for even a week. Even I, after living decades here, cannot imagine enduring again what my body once had no choice but to endure.

In those years, possessions meant nothing. Gold, jewels, diamonds—the treasures people once saved for their children's future—were suddenly worthless. A diamond ring that could once have bought a house could now only buy a single bowl of rice. Families quietly approached villagers who had been classified as "old people" and given better rations. In whispered exchanges, wealth was traded for food. For some, it was the only way to keep a child alive one more night.

But these trades were not safe. They were done in secret, hidden from Angkar's eyes. To barter was to risk everything. You never knew who you were dealing with —whether it was a hungry villager who would show mercy, or an informer ready to turn you in. If you met the wrong person, you could lose not only your diamond, but also your life. People whispered of men and women who went to trade and never came back.

I heard these stories everywhere. Diamonds passed hand to hand in the shadows, exchanged for nothing more than enough food to survive a day. When the Khmer Rouge collapsed, many villagers who had been on the receiving end of those trades emerged wealthy. But for the city people—the "new people"—the memory was one of humiliation, loss, and shame.

It was not just about food. Food was power. Angkar used hunger as its greatest weapon. To feed someone was to give them life; to deny food was to control them, punish them, even kill them without lifting a blade. Hunger was the leash, and rice was the chain.

The tragedy is that Cambodia has always been fertile. The land was capable of feeding us all. But because

Angkar hoarded and controlled the harvest, food became rarer than diamonds. It was a deliberate cruelty, a way to break the will of the "new people" and keep them in submission.

For many, there was also the haunting hope that this nightmare was temporary—that the war was over, and soon life would return to normal. That perhaps the city would reopen, markets would bustle again, families would reunite. And so they gave up their treasures for rice, holding on to life in the belief that tomorrow would be different.

But for my family and me, there was no way back. This was our home, yet it no longer felt like home. We were treated as outsiders, commodities to be used up and discarded when no longer useful. What sounded like folklore to the outside world was, for us, brutal reality. Diamonds for a bowl of rice—that was the measure of our suffering, the price of survival in Pol Pot's Cambodia.

Even today, decades later, my family laughs and says I am the easiest person to please when it comes to food. I love good, delicious meals, but I never demand, complain, or criticize what is placed before me. That is because I know the true value of food. I am grateful for every plate set before me, because I remember a time when food was more precious than gold, and when a single bowl of rice was worth more than a man's life.

And in those moments of gratitude, I remember my father's last words before he died: *"Eat what you can now, for one day you may not have the privilege to eat like this again."* At the time, I was too young to understand. But in the years that followed, as I watched people trade their diamonds for rice and others die with hunger in their eyes, I came to realize how true his words were. Food was not just nourishment. It was survival. It was dignity. It was life itself.

In those years, hunger was the true master. Angkar controlled not only our movements and our words but even the food in our mouths. For the "new people," food was the weapon most cruelly used against us. It was never enough. Starvation hollowed faces, swelled bellies, and turned strong men into skeletons.

Gold, diamonds, and family heirlooms—all the treasures carefully preserved for generations—became worthless in the face of an empty stomach. In secret, desperate families traded jewels for a few handfuls of rice. Wealth meant nothing. Hunger was the only currency that mattered.

I heard stories whispered from camp to camp. One still lingers in my heart.

There was a couple, educated and once respected, who had narrowly escaped death in the first waves of killings. They had heard the false promises that Angkar wanted people with skills from the Lon Nol government to help rebuild Cambodia. In truth, it was a trap. Those who came forward were slaughtered. Knowing this, the husband claimed he had been nothing more than a janitor in a theater, sweeping floors, cleaning seats. That lie saved his life.

But lies could not feed them. As starvation deepened, the wife took what gold they had hidden and went secretly to an "old people" village to trade for rice. She hoped to keep her husband alive. Instead, she was caught. Soldiers beat her savagely until she lost consciousness. When she awoke, she was in a place darker than death itself—the slaughterhouse.

Every night, guards escorted prisoners out of their cells. The cries, then the silence, told the truth: they were taken away to be executed. Each morning, the cells were filled again with new victims. It was a factory of death, working in silence, swallowing life after life.

But in that nightmare, a miracle of recognition occurred. One of the guards looked at her closely and realized who she was. Years earlier, he had worked for her father. He remembered the kindness he had received, the respect with which her father had treated him. That memory stirred something human in him.

Risking his own life, he whispered instructions: *Do not leave your cell tonight. Stay hidden.*

The next day, he arranged to have her transferred to a different camp. She survived there until the Vietnamese entered Cambodia and the nightmare of the Khmer Rouge ended.

When she eventually came to America, the scars of her survival remained—not only in her memory but etched into her very body. A fractured skull from the beating never fully healed. She and her husband asked me never to reveal their names. Their story is one of thousands—lives scarred, bodies broken, but survival won by the smallest threads of mercy.

Diamonds were traded for bowls of rice. Gold was traded for one more day of life. But no jewel could erase the scars.

Looking back, I see how fragile human value became under Angkar. Wealth meant nothing. Education meant nothing. Even life itself was treated as disposable. Diamonds, once treasured, could only buy a bowl of rice—and even that was a dangerous gamble.

But in the midst of that cruelty, one truth remained: kindness has a power greater than gold. A guard's memory of a father's respect saved a daughter's life. A neighbor sharing food meant another day of survival.

These acts were small in the moment, but they carried weight beyond measure.

Angkar tried to strip us of dignity, to erase humanity, to reduce us to numbers and labor. Yet these hidden moments of compassion proved that not even the darkest ideology could fully destroy the human heart. Gold and diamonds can be stolen, traded, or lost. But mercy—mercy endures.

26

BLIND WEDDING

LOVE CHOSEN BY ANGKAR, NOT BY THE HEART

IN ORDINARY TIMES, marriage in Cambodia was both a family matter and a cultural celebration. Tradition was respected, and though parents often guided the process, there was room for choice, honor, and dignity. Matchmaking was common. A family seeking a wife for their son would consult a matchmaker, someone trusted to understand the families and the young people involved. The groom's parents would present their preferences, and if the girl's family was agreeable, negotiations began.

At the heart of the agreement was the dowry. The groom's family prepared gifts—often money, gold, or items of value—meant to honor the bride's family and show the groom could provide for their daughter. If the girl's family did not favor the match, they might raise the dowry demand to unreachable levels or politely say their daughter was too young, not ready, or promised elsewhere. But always, the decision rested with the families themselves, and ultimately with the couple. A young man and woman might meet through family or community, and even if guided by tradition, they still had some power to choose whether to walk into life together.

That freedom was destroyed under Pol Pot. Angkar saw no use for romance, for heritage, for the choices of men and women. They separated us by gender—men lived in men's camps, women in women's camps—each divided again by age groups. We worked, ate, and slept apart, never allowed to meet privately, never allowed to speak of love. Any attempt at private contact between men and women was considered a crime, punishable by death.

I remember one of my colleagues who had secretly met a young woman from an "old people" village. They cared for each other in a way that was natural, human, even innocent—but Angkar saw it as rebellion. They were caught, and both were tied to poles in the center of the square, facing away from each other so they could not even exchange a glance. For days, they stood there, humiliated before us all, a living warning of what happened to those who dared to love without permission. The message was clear: *your heart does not belong to you; it belongs to Angkar.* By some mercy, my colleague was eventually released, but the scars of shame never left him.

Instead of allowing love to grow, Angkar forced marriages in the most mechanical and degrading way. Once a year, leaders lined up men and women and assigned them to one another. Sometimes hundreds of couples were matched at once. There was no asking, no courting, no choice. Refusal was not an option. To say "no" was to invite suspicion, and suspicion meant death.

After the ceremonies, Angkar arranged places for the couples to live, often in shared quarters or hastily assigned huts. It was called a "honeymoon," but it was no more than another command. What should have been sacred—two lives choosing to join together— became mechanical, stripped of intimacy, freedom, and respect.

My own sister was one of those chosen. She was matched to a man she knew in our village, but did not like him, and she accepted him because there was no choice. They built a life under those harsh beginnings, and against all odds, they remained together until he passed away recently. Their story was rare, for many couples forced into these unions lived in quiet suffering, strangers in their own homes.

Angkar did not just change marriage; they stripped it of its meaning. Love, once the heart of the family, was replaced by fear. The ancient traditions of matchmakers, dowries, and family blessings—rituals that tied generations together—were erased in a single stroke. In their place stood a system that treated men and women as pieces on a board, moved by someone else's hand.

To live under such a rule was to feel less than human. Marriage was no longer a union of hearts or a joining of families—it was simply another command of Angkar, another way to remind us that nothing in our lives, not even love, belonged to us anymore.

What made it most painful was that love, the most natural and beautiful gift of human life, had been turned into something dangerous. A glance, a smile, a word spoken in trust—any of these could lead to humiliation, punishment, or death. Under Angkar, even the heart was not free.

In the old traditions, love and marriage were tied to family, heritage, and blessing. They were imperfect, but they carried dignity and choice. Under Pol Pot, those things were erased. What remained was fear, control, and silence. And perhaps that was Angkar's deepest crime—not only to kill bodies, but to suffocate the soul, to strip away the very freedom to love.

For parents, this was the cruelest wound. To see their children handed over to strangers, stripped of choice, stripped of tenderness, stripped of the right to love—it was a nightmare. In our culture, parents had sacrificed everything for their children: working long days in the fields, saving dowries, praying for a good match. Now those dreams were replaced with fear. What could a father say to his son, or a mother to her daughter, except to whisper, *"Obey... or you will be killed"*?

And what of the marriages themselves? Some couples endured and grew close with time, even raising families together. Others lived like strangers, bound by fear but not affection. The Angkar had stolen the very heart of marriage—choice—and without choice, love became hollow. It was not two souls becoming one. It was two prisoners chained together.

This was not marriage. It was slavery dressed as tradition. It was another way Angkar sought to control not only our work and our food, but even the most sacred bond of the human heart.

Looking back, I see how deeply this cut into our culture. Marriage, once a source of joy and pride, became a reminder of fear. It taught us that even the right to love—the right to choose who to walk through life with—was no longer ours. Angkar claimed ownership of our labor, our land, our families, and now even our hearts.

I see how destructive this was—not only to couples, but to the very soul of the nation. A people who cannot choose whom to love cannot choose how to live. Angkar knew this. By controlling marriage, they controlled not only our hearts but also the generations that came after us.

Love without freedom is not love at all. Under Angkar, marriage was stripped of its joy, its dignity, and its sacredness. What should have been the most tender and personal decision of a lifetime became a decree, a command to be obeyed. The result was not families built on trust, but families bound by fear.

And yet, even in this darkness, I saw a truth: forced unions may create households, but only freedom creates true love. To love someone by choice—to give your heart freely—that is the essence of what it means to be human. Angkar tried to strip that away, but love, real love, can never be commanded.

27
CLINICS WITHOUT DOCTORS
HEALING REPLACED BY FEAR

THROUGH THE LONG years of war, we villagers endured hunger, bombings, forced labor, and endless fear. Yet one mystery still lingers in my mind: how did so many of us survive without doctors, without medicine, without the most basic care?

In America, I see people spend enormous sums on health care, gyms, diets, and cosmetic products— chasing wellness, even beauty. And yet, even with all the advances, many fall sick. In Cambodia under Pol Pot, we had nothing—no hospitals, no medicines, no hygiene products—and yet somehow, we endured. Perhaps it was fear itself that kept people alive. Because to show sickness was to risk your life. A weak body meant you might be judged unfit for labor, and those who could not work were discarded.

The slogan rang through loudspeakers, echoed in meetings, carved into our minds like a knife:

"No gain to keep you, no loss to kill you."

We were not people in their eyes. We were tools. If useful, we lived. If not, we were thrown away.

I remember infections that tormented me—my leg swelled so badly I nearly lost it, my teeth throbbed with pain until my face ballooned. There was no dentist, no medicine, no relief but endurance. To admit weakness was to invite suspicion, and suspicion was often a death sentence. Our bodies wore down like old machines, but still we were forced to march to the fields.

One day, I collapsed at work. I remember nothing of it. Later, they told me I was loaded onto a wagon pulled by two cows and hauled for hours along rough roads to what they called a "clinic." In truth, it was not a hospital at all. It was a pagoda—a Buddhist temple— stripped of monks and consecrated life, now converted into a ward for the dying.

The rooms where monks had once chanted prayers were filled with thin, frail bodies. The smell of sickness hung in the air. There were no doctors, because Pol Pot had killed them all. Instead, Angkar trained women with little knowledge, whose only tools were large needles and vials of a mysterious liquid. That was their cure. That was their medicine.

Each morning and evening, patients lined up for the same injection, no matter what illness they had. The same liquid for a cough, for fever, for infection, for collapse. One by one, we rolled up our sleeves, waiting for the sting of the needle. Over time, our skin hardened, our muscles bruised. Fear of the injection itself became part of our sickness. It was not healing—it was ritual, a show of control.

I lay unconscious for three days. I should have died. But when I awoke, my mother was there. She had come because the wagon passed near her village, and someone told her it was me. She begged permission to stay and care for me, and by some miracle, they allowed it. When I tried to rise, she pressed me gently back down. I was too frail to stand. She whispered that many believed I would never wake again. But God had spared me. It was a miracle of grace, unexplainable in such a place of death.

Recovery, however, was nearly impossible. My body was fragile, desperately in need of real nourishment— but food was scarce. Even in the clinic, meals were thin and inadequate, as though Angkar used starvation as another form of purging. We were not encouraged to rest or heal; we were hurried back to the fields as soon as we could stand. Conversation was forbidden. We were told to smile and nod as if everything was fine, even when death was only a breath away.

In that silence, one act of mercy gave me hope. I had a cousin who had married a man adopted by a Chinese couple. He spoke fluent Chinese, and because of that, he was considered "old people" and spared. But my cousin and her two small children—a beautiful five-year-old girl and a three-year-old boy—were not. They were executed as Chinese. Only he survived. In his grief, he sought me out and quietly introduced me to one of the nurses. By this small connection, she took pity on me.

Each evening, when no one was watching, she would slip leftover food into a dark room. At night, I would go there to collect it. It was never much, but it was a precious gift—life itself hidden in scraps. That food gave me the strength to hold on.

Until one night. In the darkness, I stepped on a rotten floorboard. It snapped beneath me, and I fell, breaking my ankle. The bone never healed properly, and to this day, it still protrudes from my left foot. That was the last time I went back for food.

The clinic was no place of healing. It was a place where the sick were watched, injected, and left to die. Patients disappeared quietly, without investigation, without mourning. To ask questions was to risk your own life.

This was the best care Angkar offered—temples turned to death houses, nurses turned to enforcers, injections turned to instruments of fear. But in the midst of it, I tasted both the cruelty of man and the quiet mercy of God. I should not have lived. Yet I did. And every scar on my body tells the story of that survival.

What haunts me most is that these places of suffering were once sacred. The very walls that had echoed with Buddhist chants and prayers for peace now echoed with silence, fear, and the groans of the dying. Pagodas, once symbols of community, faith, and rest, became graveyards of the living.

Pol Pot's regime not only tried to break our bodies; it tried to erase our souls. It stripped away mercy, care, and compassion until even healing was replaced by fear. To survive was not only a physical act, but a spiritual defiance—a refusal to let death have the last word.

28

SCATTERED FOR SLAUGHTER
UNITY WAS A THREAT

I DO NOT REMEMBER the exact year. By then, time was no longer marked by calendars but by the rhythm of survival—days of hunger, nights of fear, and the rare week each year when I was allowed to come home. Even then, I hardly saw my siblings. Each of us had been scattered into different labor groups, fighting our own lonely battles to survive. Home was no longer a place of family, but a shell of memory.

One day, news spread through whispers: Angkar had given an order. All Chinese who had been living among the "new people" were to be relocated. At first, it sounded like good news. We were told this meant we would live with the "old people," those who still enjoyed a measure of stability and food. Some celebrated, believing it was the long-promised reward Angkar had spoken of during the war.

But I felt no joy. Deep inside, suspicion burned. I had learned not to trust Angkar's gifts. What looked like an opportunity often hid the shadow of death. And I feared this was not an upgrade, but a trap.

The truth became clear soon enough. Families were broken apart. Each person was assigned to a new destination, separated from those they knew, sent off alone or in small groups. To scatter was Angkar's way of eliminating unity. A people bound together—by family, culture, or shared history—were a threat. But scattered and isolated, they became easier to control, easier to erase.

Even in our own village, we saw it unfold. This time, it was only my mother and my older brother, who still lived at home, who were relocated. The rest of us—my siblings and I—were never informed. Angkar did not ask, and we had no right to know. Only after it was done did we hear what had happened to them. We could not help, could not ask questions, could not resist. Families did not simply move; they were torn apart with silence.

For the Chinese among us, this scattering was especially dangerous. We were rebranded again and again: once privileged, then demoted, then promised privilege once more. Each label was a mask that hid the same intention—division and silent elimination. Some never returned from their new destinations. Others simply disappeared without a word.

We did not need guns or mass executions to see what was happening. It was slaughtered by scattering. It was death by design, disguised as relocation.

I remember hiding my Chinese books on the rooftop of our house, tucking them away where no one could find them. They were my secret treasure—the only reminder of a world of learning and identity that Angkar was trying to erase. Whenever I managed to slip home from the camp, I would steal moments to climb up, retrieve them, and study in silence—my heart racing at every sound outside, fearful of discovery. Those books gave me a sense of dignity, of worth, of being more than just another body in the fields.

But in time, even that small treasure was lost. I never had the chance to bring them back with me again. Perhaps to others they would have seemed worthless— just paper and ink—but to me they were life. My family had already lost so much. And now, even the little we held onto was stripped away once more by Angkar's hand.

On the surface, they told us we were being sent to live among the "old people." It sounded like relocation, even integration. But beneath that surface, danger was always waiting. Relocation was not mercy—it was a strategy of scattering, of weakening, of erasing. Every move was another step closer to disappearance.

For many Chinese families, that journey would be their last. They packed what little they had left—some clothes, a pot, a few memories—and walked toward an unknown fate. Death followed quietly behind them, needing no reason, no justification. It came in the night, in the fields, in the silence between orders.

I began to sense what I could not yet speak aloud: death was near, and there would be no escape. Angkar scattered us not to save us, but to erase us—body, name, and memory.

From that moment, every sunrise felt borrowed. Each day was a gift that could be taken without warning. We no longer dreamed of tomorrow—we only prayed to survive the night.

29
DEATH WAS NEAR AND NO ESCAPE
THE SENTENCE WITHOUT A CRIME

I DO NOT REMEMBER EXACTLY how it happened, but somehow my family was allowed to return to our own house in the village. The barn was gone, but the house still stood—thanks to our neighbors, who loved us enough to keep watch over it until we returned.

When I stepped inside, the air felt different. It carried the scent of earth and wood that I had known since childhood. The worn walls and the familiar corners seemed to welcome us back, whispering, *You still belong here.* For a brief moment, it was as if the years of terror and displacement had dissolved, and we had returned to a life before the storm.

Sitting once again in the house of my youth, I felt a sense of belonging I had almost forgotten. Memories of laughter, family meals, and the warmth of ordinary days flooded back. The simple act of being home—of seeing the same trees, the same yard, the same paths where I had once played as a boy—gave me a fleeting glimpse of the world we had lost.

It was a good memory, a fragile mercy in the midst of chaos. For a few moments, it felt as though the clock had turned back and life might one day be normal again. But deep down, I knew this joy was borrowed time, and the shadow of Angkar still loomed.

The joy was short-lived. What had felt like a miracle—returning to the house of my childhood, the one our neighbors had kept safe—was only the first act of a cruel play. Not long after we settled back among familiar walls and the scent of earth and wood, Angkar spoke a sentence that changed everything: the Chinese would no longer be allowed to live in Cambodia.

They declared us a burden to the "pure" future Pol Pot imagined. Our names, our faces, the language in our mouths—things we had never chosen—became the proof of our guilt. There was no trial and no accusation that fitted a crime; the crime was simply who we were. It was ethnic cleansing, and it arrived not with explanations but with a decree.

We waited. Waiting became a new kind of torment. I had survived bombs and fever, hunger and endless backbreaking labor; I had known the ache of loss and the hollow of fear. But this was different. This was a sentence written against our existence. The leaders told us to remain at home. Soldiers watched every path. Neighbors wept silently at our door and came to say goodbye as if we were already dead. Their faces held sorrow—and a helpless resignation that stung worse than any insult. Love from them could not bend the law.

Rumors arrived first as whispers on the wind: entire families gone, houses emptied overnight, cries cut off in the dark. Then one morning, we heard for ourselves: families from nearby villages had been taken. Some never returned. Children. Mothers. Grandfathers. The killing moved like a slow, efficient tide—one village, then the next—leaving silence where life had been noisy and ordinary.

In that week, I could not eat. My mouth would not shape words. I sat and stared until my eyes burned with tears I could not let fall. I remember lifting my face to the sky and asking God—if there was an answer—to hear me. I was not afraid of work, hunger, or pain; I had known all those things before. But the nearness of death—ordered, final, and without reason—hollowed me out. Time lost its measure and quickened at once; each day closed in like a tightening noose.

At night, the village sounded different. The wind carried muffled gunfire and the wet, terrible sounds of people being taken. We could hear the cries that came from other homes while our own house remained full of silence. Every dawn promised a new rupture—another family gone, another yard emptied, another cart of belongings abandoned on the road.

For days, I sat with that silence and listened to the old teaching echo in my mind: that life is a circle, that each suffering must be paid for in another life, that karma balances the books of the world. Around me, villagers murmured the same thing—the old comforts returned in whispers. When a child died, someone would say, *it was his fate from a past life.* When a family starved, they murmured, *perhaps they owed this debt.* The words were meant to soothe, to give shape to senseless pain. They were a map for a world that had no other explanation.

But as the soldiers watched our house and the rumor of our end drew near, those words stopped bringing comfort and began to cut. I found myself trapped between two answers. On one side was the quiet, patient resignation of my people: accept your suffering, maybe the next life will be kinder. On the other side was a wild, young anger—not against the men with guns, but against fate itself. I kept asking: if this is my karma, then why must the innocent suffer? If the work of our hands was honest, if our lives had been given to the land and to our neighbors, could all of that be erased by a single decree?

In those sleepless nights, I wrestled with questions too heavy for my age. The teachings I had grown up hearing about patience and destiny no longer satisfied the ache inside me. I wanted to believe that goodness still mattered, that there was justice somewhere beyond the reach of Angkar's power. Yet all around me, good people were dying, and the wicked seemed untouchable. I felt the pull between surrender and resistance— between faith and despair.

It was in that quiet war inside my heart that I began to understand: when a nation loses its soul, every man must choose whether to let his own be taken too.

Sometimes I tried to reason it away. Perhaps some wrong in a former life had returned to settle its score. Perhaps this hardship was meant to teach. But the more I tried to shape those thoughts into peace, the less they fit the reality that stared me in the face: a brutal, political hatred that had nothing to do with cosmic justice. This was not a private reckoning between a soul and its past; this was a deliberate, public erasure.

At night, I remember lying awake and thinking of the many small kindnesses that made up my life—the neighbor who shared rice with another neighbor, the teacher who once bowed when I first learned to read a letter, the monk who blessed my sibling at birth. If karma was a ledger, none of those acts should have been so easily outweighed. I could not reconcile a moral calculus so cold with the warmth of human ties I had known.

In that liminal place between waiting and fearing, another thought pushed through the old beliefs: could prayer change the account? I lifted my eyes to the sky and did something I had not done before with a full heart—I asked. Not for a grand sign, not for explanations, but for mercy. If the law of rebirth was true, then I prayed that mercy might find its way into the balance. If it was not, then I prayed to a God I had only recently begun to trust, begging that He would not let my life end as a meaningless tally.

This tug—between the ancestral comfort of karma and the urgent pleading of my own soul—became one of the deepest tests of those days. Some nights, I surrendered to resignation because it felt safer than hope. Other nights, I held fast to a rebel's belief that destiny could be overturned, that love and memory could outrun a decree.

Yet prayer did not shield me from sorrow. Not long after, word came of my cousin who lived in the nearby town. She and her husband had two children—a little girl of five, beautiful and bright, and a boy of three, full of laughter and life. Her husband, Cambodian by blood but adopted by a Chinese family from infancy, spoke fluent Chinese. That detail, meant to be a blessing of belonging, became the weight of their undoing. They were among the first group of Chinese to be taken to the slaughter.

My heart broke with grief and terror. I knew then that my own family could be next in line. Her husband survived, not because of mercy, but because of origin —his blood marked him as Cambodian. He later told me how he begged them to spare his children, to let them live, even if he could not raise them. But his plea was refused. The children were taken, and he walked away alone, carrying a wound that has never healed. He is the only one alive today.

It was the most inhuman treatment I had ever witnessed. To strip parents of their children, to extinguish lives so innocent and full of promise, was cruelty beyond comprehension. And yet, it was the reality of Angkar's design—a system that counted lives as nothing, that shattered families without hesitation, that left survivors burdened with memories too heavy to bear.

In the end, neither certainty nor comfort came by human calculation. What followed was not the simple payment of a past due, nor the slow unfolding of an inevitable fate. It was something stranger and more dangerous—a mercy I did not expect, and a reprieve that I could not explain at the time.

Angkar could kill the body, but it could not silence the cries of the brokenhearted.

30

LIVES WERE SPARED, BUT DANGER REMAINED

HOPE IN THE SHADOW OF DEATH

I BELIEVE with all my heart that there is a God who hears the cries of His creation. The blood of the innocent had risen to heaven, and somehow, mercy reached us. Just as death was inching closer, Angkar gave the order to stop the killing before it reached my village.

When the village leader came to deliver the news, I could hardly believe it. His words sounded like a dream, too good to be true. For days, I had sat in silence, convinced that death was certain. Now I was told I would live. It was as though the sun had risen after endless nights of darkness.

I knew at that moment that my life had been spared for a reason. I vowed not to waste it. Whatever the future held, I would face it with all my strength. I no longer feared what tomorrow might bring, for God had given me back my today.

But Angkar's mercy was not without cruelty. Along with the reprieve came new orders. The young people, like my siblings and me, were to be sent away—not to execution, but to the death camps. There, Angkar reasoned, it was not necessary to kill us quickly. Instead, we would be worked until death, starved and broken. In their minds, it was more efficient: the labor of our bodies could be harvested before our lives were extinguished.

My siblings and I braced ourselves for this new fate. We reported to the village leader, waiting to be assigned to one of the camps. To our astonishment, he quietly redirected us. Instead of sending us to the death camps, he placed us in different labor camps for the "old people." It was an act of extraordinary courage, for he risked his own life to spare ours. He had known our family all his life, and in that moment, he chose to help us in the only way he could.

For me, the assignment felt like the best job I had been given under Angkar. Caring for the buffaloes and the wagon, fetching water for the Old People's camp — the work was grueling, but compared with the fields and the construction sites, it was a blessing: I finally had enough to eat and my body, starved for years, found a small measure of strength again. Still, the comfort was brittle. When I went to the leader who gave me the post, I was shocked to discover I was not out of danger. He handed me two huge buffaloes —

one of them blind in an eye — and grinned as if to warn me. In Cambodia, we say someone is "stubborn like a blind buffalo," and that was the look he gave me: a test and a threat all at once. Then he added the real warning: if the wagon under my care were ever to break, Angkar would take my life, for a broken wagon meant I had become the enemy of Angkar. It was almost a death sentence by itself — for how could I keep heavy wheels from sinking and snapping on the rutted, muddy roads we were forced to use? Even in a place that felt easier, fear rode with me every mile.

This was my last job before Pol Pot's regime collapsed. It was the work that sustained me until liberation came.

Later, I met a friend who had not been as fortunate. He was sent to a death camp—a place where life had no meaning and mercy was unknown. When he told me what he had endured, I realized just how miraculous my survival had been.

He had lost everything. His parents were gone, his older brother—weak from malaria—had been left behind to rest, and his younger brother and two little sisters vanished with them. Only he and four of his older siblings survived that day, spared not because of strength or strategy, but because Angkar suddenly changed its mind and stopped the executions at the last moment. They were part of a Chinese group marked for death, and that unexpected decision had drawn the line between life and death.

The rest were sent to the death camp from which no one returned. My friend described it as a place of endless torment—men and women driven to the brink, starving, collapsing in the fields, punished for weakness, working until their bodies gave out. It was cruelty beyond words, cruelty designed to erase life slowly and silently.

He told me that the camp held not only Chinese families but also Cambodians whom Angkar accused of crimes, real or imagined. Very few ever came out alive. Those who did owed their survival to the arrival of the Vietnamese soldiers who liberated the camps. Without that invasion, my friend said, none of them would have lived to tell their stories.

I listened, and my heart broke. That could have been me. That should have been me. But I was spared. And for the rest of my life, I would carry both the weight of that miracle and the sorrow of those who did not live to see freedom.

Looking back, I know this was mercy—mercy that still existed even in the darkest corners of the world. It was with mercy that Angkar stopped the killing before it reached our village. It was mercy that the leader, at great personal risk, sent my siblings and me to safer camps instead of the death camps. It was mercy that I was given work that kept me alive when so many others were worked to death.

In a time when despair seemed like the only honest response, I had to choose instead to hold on to these fragments of grace. If I focused only on the killings, the lies, and the cruelty, I would have drowned in hopelessness. But when I lifted my eyes to see what had been spared—the chance to live another day, the courage of one man to help us, the food that gave me strength—I found enough to carry on.

Mercy does not erase tragedy. It does not undo the graves that lined our land or the cries that haunted our nights. But it does shine, even if faintly, through the cracks of a broken world. And when it came to me, I clung to it with everything I had.

That mercy was not just for survival. It was a reminder that even in a world ruled by fear, cruelty, and death, compassion had not been extinguished completely. It lived in the choices of neighbors who cared for us, in the courage of leaders who quietly protected us, and in the mysterious providence that allowed me to live when others did not.

It taught me this: to survive was not simply to endure. It was to see the good, however small, and let it anchor your heart when everything else tried to tear it apart.

I came to understand that my life was spared for a reason. I refused to let Angkar decide when my story would end. As long as I still had breath, I still had the will to live. Even the smallest hope was enough to give me strength. Like a single light shining in the vast darkness, it guided me when everything around me seemed lost. That faint, flickering light became my compass, reminding me that as long as there was life, there was purpose—and as long as there was purpose, there was still a way forward.

But even light, when surrounded by darkness, must fight to survive. The days that followed would test that light more than ever before.

31
HUNTER TURNED HUNTED
WHEN THE TIDE FINALLY SHIFTED

WE HAD SUFFERED beyond what our bodies could endure. Hunger, exhaustion, disease, and endless labor had stripped us down to skin and bone. Our minds, too, were battered daily by the slogans that blasted from the loudspeakers—harsh words echoing over the fields, drilled into our ears until we thought we might go insane. "No gain to keep you, no loss to kill you." "The weak branch must be cut." Over and over, the voice of Angkar haunted our thoughts, as if trying to convince us that we were already less than human.

And yet, in the middle of all that despair, we clung to one fragile thread: hope. It was not a strong hope, not something we could clearly see. It was more like a faint whisper, a small rational thought that maybe—just maybe—one day something would happen to change our fate.

Then, the rumors began.

Something strange was happening among the leaders. The men who once strutted with boldness, fierce in their commands and quick with threats, now seemed reserved, even nervous. Their eyes betrayed a worry they tried to hide. They no longer shouted with the same fire. Their steps were less sure. Whispers passed from villager to villager: *Something is happening.*

Then, from a distance, came the sound—like thunder rolling across the horizon, but sharper, heavier. Bombs. At first, far away, then each day closer. Each explosion cracked the air like a promise that the world was shifting.

And then, the impossible happened. The most notorious leaders—the very ones who had spilled the most blood, who had terrified us into silence—began to run. Word spread quickly that villagers, those who had lost entire families to these men, seized their chance. Years of grief and rage erupted. They hunted their hunters. Some leaders were dragged down and beaten, some killed on the spot. It was as if the strongest tiger of the jungle had finally been wounded, and the hyenas who once trembled before him now tore him apart.

For the first time in years, the tide had turned. The fear we carried every day was mirrored in the faces of the Khmer Rouge themselves. Liberation was near.

For my siblings and me, there was only one thought: get home. We hurried back to reunite with one another, clinging to what little family we had left. We did not join the killing sprees—we had seen enough blood, enough vengeance. Instead, we stayed close, waited, and watched.

The air was electric with chaos. Leaders ran into the forests they once commanded, and people chased them like prey. Villagers who had once bowed in silence now raised their voices in anger. But we were cautious. In the past, rumors of freedom had surfaced, only to be crushed by a swift return of Angkar's power. Many who had dared to believe before had been slaughtered for their courage.

So we did not celebrate openly. We waited. We listened. We watched for the truth.

Still, the forest was their home. The Khmer Rouge had always been strongest in the shadows, skilled at survival in the jungles. They vanished back into their hiding places, regrouping, their presence lingering like a sickness not yet cured. Angkar was wounded, yes, but not dead. And we knew—wounded animals are often the most dangerous.

The moment was both liberation and warning. Hope had broken through the darkness, but danger still surrounded us. The hunters had been hunted—but the hunt was not yet over.

As we watched the Khmer Rouge scatter, a strange tension filled the air. For years, we had longed for this moment—for the day when those who tormented us would themselves be driven into fear. And yet, when it finally came, the feeling was not pure joy. It was guarded, heavy, and complicated.

We remembered 1975. We remembered how the streets of Phnom Penh had once been filled with celebration, people waving flags and cheering, believing that peace had come at last. We remembered the smiling faces, the relief, the hope that the nightmare of war was finally over. But that day of celebration became the doorway into hell. What we thought was freedom was only the beginning of the killing fields.

That memory haunted us now. We had learned the hard way that not every "liberation" leads to life. This time, we were more cautious. We dared not dance in the streets, dared not raise our voices too loudly. Instead, we whispered our hopes in private, our joy muted by fear. Yes, the hunters had become the hunted, but who would rise in their place? Who would rule tomorrow? No one knew.

The situation was fluid, uncertain. Rumors ran faster than the truth. Some said new leaders had emerged, others said foreign armies were moving in. Still others warned that the Khmer Rouge would regroup and return, angrier than before. Every story carried both relief and danger. We had survived long enough to know that in Cambodia, power could change in an instant—and with it, life or death.

The sound grew louder with each passing day—an unrelenting rhythm that echoed through the forest and across the plains. But this time, it was not the echo of commands or the crack of executions; it was the thunder of something greater, something foreign yet strangely familiar. The rumble came from the main highway that led toward the city—toward Siem Reap. To us, that road had always been a path of fear, but now it carried a different sound, a different promise.

Each explosion in the distance told us that something was shifting. Hell itself was breaking apart. We could feel it in the trembling of the earth beneath our feet, taste it in the dust that hung in the air. The nightmare that had swallowed our lives was cracking open.

Whispers spread through the villages: *Angkar is losing.* We saw the once-proud leaders flee into the forests, abandoning their posts, their weapons, even their slogans. The faces that once looked upon us with power now vanished into the trees, chased by the very terror they had sown.

For the first time in years, joy began to stir—not loud or careless, but deep and trembling. Could this be real? Could freedom truly be near? Our hearts dared to hope again. The war drums that once signaled death now sounded like the heartbeat of deliverance.

And as the mortar fire rolled closer each day, we knew —this time, it was not the end of life, but the beginning of it. The flame of hope we had guarded so carefully through the darkness was no longer fragile; it was alive, burning steady, and leading us toward a new dawn.

32

MASTER RETURNS TO SETTLE THE SCORE: THE APPRENTICE OVERTHROWN BY THE MASTER

THE APPRENTICE OVERTHROWN BY THE MASTER

WHEN THE KHMER ROUGE first took power, few people understood how deeply their rise had been tied to the Viet Cong. During the long years of war, it was Vietnamese soldiers who had trained them, armed them, and guided them through jungle warfare. The Khmer Rouge learned tactics, discipline, and political indoctrination from their Vietnamese mentors, who had themselves spent decades fighting foreign powers. Yet when Lon Nol's government finally collapsed in April 1975, and Cambodia fell completely into Khmer Rouge hands, the Vietnamese were nowhere to be seen in the victory parades. They had been erased from the story —betrayed by those they had once empowered. Not a single record or speech acknowledged their role in the revolution. Pol Pot and his inner circle claimed the triumph as their own, rewriting history to make the

Khmer Rouge appear self-born, pure, and independent of all foreign influence.

Pol Pot and his circle, obsessed with building a "pure Cambodia," turned on their former allies. They stirred up riots against the Vietnamese, driving them out. The Khmer Rouge wanted no master above them, no shadow of foreign influence to remind them of their past dependence. The Vietnamese withdrew, humiliated and bitter, but they did not forget.

I was young then and knew little of politics. But even I could sense that this betrayal had planted a deep wound between master and apprentice. Years later, when cracks began to form within Pol Pot's leadership, that wound opened wide—and this time, it was the master who returned to settle the score.

For us villagers, it was liberation. The Vietnamese came not in whispers, not as hidden guests in the countryside, but as an army. No longer called Viet Cong, they now marched openly as Vietnamese soldiers. They came with tanks rumbling along the highways, trucks packed with troops, and motorbikes roaring through clouds of dust. They did not sneak into villages under the cover of night; they thundered down the main roads toward Phnom Penh and other cities with force and certainty.

To us, their arrival felt like the breaking of a curse. We were so desperate for deliverance that we no longer cared what banner it came under. Our bodies were frail, our spirits crushed, and our souls weary from years of cruelty under the Angkar. We had been stripped of everything—dignity, hope, even the will to dream. So when the first signs of liberation reached our ears, it felt like a miracle. Whether foreign or local, known or unknown, it did not matter who brought it. All we wanted was freedom—to breathe again, to live without fear, and to see the end of the nightmare that had turned our nation into the Killing Fields.

Our village lay far from the main highway, so we did not see them with our own eyes. But we heard the news spreading like fire. Within weeks, the Vietnamese had entered the cities and toppled Pol Pot's government. The once-proud hunters, who had ruled us with slogans and fear, now fled like prey into the forests they once called home.

It was not the end of danger. The Khmer Rouge were not destroyed. They still prowled in the shadows, clashing with Vietnamese and government soldiers, waging guerrilla warfare. Sometimes their battles came so close to our villages that we could hear the gunfire. People still lived in fear of them, for though their power was broken, their cruelty remained.

But something had changed. The air was different. We were no longer completely alone. The Vietnamese came as deliverers, as liberators, and—for a time—as rulers. They held the cities, restored a measure of order, and brought us back from the edge of total death.

The master had returned to settle the score with the apprentice, but the scars of betrayal, bloodshed, and hunger were still carved deep into our land and our lives. Liberation had come, yet healing was still far away.

But though the Khmer Rouge had been broken, their shadow still haunted Cambodia. Pol Pot and his men melted back into the forests—the very ground where their revolution had first taken root. They were wounded, but not destroyed. Their presence lingered like a sickness in the air—unseen, yet always near, always threatening to strike again.

For ordinary people like us, the Vietnamese advance meant survival, but not yet peace. We lived in the uneasy space between deliverance and danger, between the relief of being spared and the fear that the night-mare could return at any moment.

And yet, when liberation finally reached us, it was like the final wall of darkness cracking open to let in the light. I had endured hunger, sickness, forced labor, and the constant shadow of death. My body had been worn down, but it was my soul that was most fragile— so brittle that it felt it would not take much more before it shattered completely.

So when freedom came, I did not care who the liberators were or what flag they carried. All I knew was this: I was free. Free from the endless slogans. Free from the constant fear of execution. Free from the hopeless cycle of working only toward death.

For the first time in years, I breathed without chains around my chest. And though the road ahead was uncertain, though the land was scarred and the people broken, I tasted something I had almost forgotten —hope.

Cambodia as a whole could not have continued under Pol Pot's brutal grip. It had to be stopped. Liberation carried a cost, but it was the only path forward. Healing would take years—perhaps generations—but in that moment, the simple truth of freedom was enough.

We who had lived under Angkar had stopped using our God-given minds to think, to dream, or to plan. We only obeyed. Now, suddenly, we were free to choose again. Free to wonder what tomorrow could hold. And yet, even as joy surged, part of me could not fully believe it. Could it really be true? Could it last?

It would take me time to digest this freedom, to trust that it was real. But one thing was certain: the nightmare of Pol Pot's rule had ended. Liberation had come.

PART FOUR
LIBERATION AND EXILE

33
WHEN THE WALLS CRUMBLED
VIETNAMESE ARMIES LIBERATE
CAMBODIA

WHEN THE KHMER ROUGE seized power in 1975, the joy of victory was muted, almost hollow. The people celebrated because the war had ended, but beneath the cheers lay suspicion, unease, and skepticism. We had no reason to trust the new rulers. And in time, our fears were proven right—Pol Pot's Angkar turned celebration into slaughter, and the promises of peace into more than four years of living hell.

Those years seemed endless, as though time itself had stopped. Every day was the same routine of hunger, labor, slogans, and fear. It felt as if we lived outside the normal flow of history—trapped in an eternity of torment where the days did not pass, but only repeated.

But then, the Vietnamese came. Their armies pushed into Cambodia, and the walls of Pol Pot's tyranny crumbled. For the first time in years, we felt the weight lift. Liberation had come. The cruel voices that once blasted from loudspeakers fell silent. No more orders to bow, no more threats echoing across the fields. For the first time, we could breathe.

The joy was real this time. We smiled without fear, laughed without shame, and slept without nightmares of being dragged away in the night. We celebrated not with fireworks or parades, but with simple acts of freedom—sleeping late, waking without fear, eating without trembling that someone would take our food away. After so many years of darkness, even the smallest freedoms felt like miracles.

And yet, beneath the joy came a strange new reality. For years, Angkar had controlled every detail of our lives. We had not been allowed to think for ourselves, to plan, to dream. Now suddenly, we were free—but freedom required choices, decisions, responsibility. After so many years of being treated as tools, our minds were stiff, like unused muscles. We had forgotten how to think about the future.

For poor villagers like us, survival had always depended on traditions passed down from our fathers and mothers—how to plant rice, how to build shelters, how to care for animals. But Angkar had ripped those traditions apart. Families had been separated, elders silenced, knowledge lost. Now we were like children set loose in a world that had changed, with no map to guide us.

The Vietnamese had liberated us, but they could not heal us. They could not erase the scars carved into our hearts or restore the trust that Pol Pot had shattered. That would take time. Healing would take more than soldiers and tanks; it would take courage, patience, and faith.

But for now, in those first days after liberation, we did not think of the future. We only lived in the moment, grateful that we had survived the eternity of hell, grateful that the walls of Angkar had finally crumbled.

Freedom had come, but freedom alone was not enough. We had been broken, silenced, and stripped of the very skills and traditions that once guided our lives. Liberation tore down the walls of fear, but inside those ruins, we still had to learn how to stand again.

Yet as I looked back, the contrast between this moment and the "liberation" of 1975 burned in my mind. When the Khmer Rouge first entered Phnom Penh, there were cheers in the streets, fireworks of hope that the long war was over. But that celebration quickly turned to ashes. What had seemed like freedom became slavery. What had been hailed as victory became our undoing.

This time, when Pol Pot's walls collapsed, the joy was different. It was deep, but it was cautious. It was almost unreal, as if we were afraid to believe it. Could it truly be over? Could the nightmare finally end? Liberation felt like light bursting through a cracked wall—blinding, unfamiliar, almost too strong for eyes that had lived in darkness for so long.

We stumbled into freedom like prisoners who had forgotten how to walk. The open sky felt strange. The silence of the slogans was almost unsettling. After years of being told what to think, what to say, what to do, I no longer knew how to use my own mind. My thoughts were crippled by fear, my heart still braced for the sound of boots, the call of Angkar, the whistle that summoned us to work or to death.

Even though I was free, I was more fearful of the future than I had ever been. The unknown stretched before me like a vast, empty field. How would I start again? How would any of us? Families were broken, skills lost, traditions disrupted, faith in one another shattered. The Vietnamese armies had driven away the hunters, but they could not restore what Angkar had taken from our families, our culture, and our hearts.

So we gave ourselves time. Time to breathe. Time to recover from the shock of watching everything turn upside down in a single moment. Time to let the reality sink in that somehow—without warning—we were alive, and we were free.

In those first days of freedom, joy and fear lived side by side in our hearts. We rejoiced that Angkar's grip had finally been broken, but the question of tomorrow lingered like a shadow. Could a nation so wounded ever truly heal? Could people so conditioned to silence ever find their voices again?

I realized then that freedom was not the end of the story—it was the beginning of a harder journey. Liberation gave us space to live, but healing would require courage to face our pain, patience to rebuild what was lost, and faith to believe that life could hold more than survival.

For some, especially the *old people* who had been favored under the Angkar, this new dawn came with uncertainty. During Pol Pot's regime, they had been elevated above others—not by merit or wisdom, but by classification. Their positions, though often hollow, had given them food, privilege, and a fragile sense of importance in a world ruled by fear. Now that the system had collapsed and a new government was forming under Vietnamese guidance, their fortune was reversed. The future held no guarantees, and for some, life under the old rule—even in its cruelty—had offered more stability than the unknown that awaited.

Yet, despite these mixed feelings, the air carried something no one could deny: a sense of release. The shouts of joy, the quiet tears, the songs that returned to the lips of weary people—all spoke of a nation awakening from a long nightmare. For now, everyone—young and old, broken and burdened—shared one common truth: the Killing Fields were behind us.

The walls of Angkar had crumbled, but the walls inside of us—the fear, the mistrust, the scars—would take years to fall. And yet, even in that fragile beginning, there was one undeniable truth: we were alive, and we were free. That was enough to start again.

But freedom, as we would soon learn, was only the first battle. Rebuilding life from the ashes would test our strength in ways we had never imagined.

34

THE NEW PEOPLE RISE AND
THE OLD REMAIN
KNOWLEDGE CANNOT BE KILLED

UNDER POL POT, the *New People* were branded as enemies of the revolution. We were mocked, starved, and stripped of all dignity, as though our lives carried no worth. Many of us had once been teachers, students, or skilled workers, but to survive, we had to bury our past. Some pretended to be simple farmers, forcing their hands to blister in the fields and their minds to grow quiet. Others faked ignorance, stumbling over simple words so as not to appear educated. In a world where knowledge had become a death sentence, pretending to be foolish was the only wisdom left.

Angkar's pursuit of those who had once held rank under the Lon Nol government never ceased. Their spies listened in the shadows, their informants watched every movement. It was only a matter of time before someone was found out.

One day, our village was summoned for a "special meeting." Attendance was mandatory. We gathered in the open clearing, uncertain of what was to come. But it soon became clear that this was no meeting—it was an execution. Angkar had discovered that one man among us had hidden his true identity, a former official who had managed to survive by blending in as a farmer. He was called out before the crowd, his name spoken like an accusation.

Without trial, without a word of defense, he was shot in front of us. The sound of the gunfire shattered the silence, and in that instant, time itself seemed to stop. No one screamed, no one moved. We stood frozen— our hearts pounding, our minds reeling with horror. The message was unmistakable: *Angkar sees all. There is no escape.*

From that day on, fear lived with us like a shadow. We learned to speak less, to think less, to hope less. And yet, deep inside, one truth could not be erased: knowledge cannot be killed. They could silence voices, burn books, and bury the wise—but truth, once known, would always find a way to rise again.

But Angkar's propaganda was not the full truth. It could strip us of dignity, but it could not erase knowledge. It could take away books, jobs, and property, but it could not kill the mind.

When the Vietnamese armies liberated Cambodia, the truth began to surface. The *New People*, long discarded as useless, began to rise from the ashes. Doctors, teachers, professors, businessmen, and women who had once been forced to hide their knowledge now stepped back into the light. They returned to their former professions, and slowly, the lifeless rhythm of the nation began to stir again. Streets that had been empty for years filled once more with footsteps and the hum of conversation. Markets reopened, colors returned, and the sound of commerce replaced the silence of fear. Those who had once begged for mercy now stood with the authority to grant it.

Yet for many, returning home was not an easy decision. The cities they had been driven out of had stood abandoned since the day Angkar ordered their evacuation. Houses, offices, warehouses—all lay frozen in time, untouched and unclaimed. The buildings were still there, but they were hollow, haunted by memories of those who had vanished.

When the survivors finally dared to return, they came with mixed feelings—grief, wonder, and disbelief. They walked through streets where grass had grown through the cracks of pavement, through neighborhoods where silence had replaced laughter. And as they reclaimed what had once been theirs, some found themselves surrounded by absence. Their neighbors were gone, their families scattered or dead.

In that vacuum, opportunity grew. Many reclaimed their old homes and businesses; others took possession of what once belonged to those who never returned. Some grew wealthy overnight—not through ambition or deceit, but through the strange mercy of survival. The world had been turned upside down, and those who once lived in ashes now found themselves standing amid the ruins of a kingdom waiting to be rebuilt.

Not all survived. Many brilliant minds were silenced forever in the Killing Fields. But those who endured showed the power of knowledge. The villagers who had been elevated by the Khmer Rouge—the so-called Old People—were left exposed. Their wealth and power had not come from merit, but from Angkar's system of fear. When freedom returned, that false power crumbled.

For villagers like us, however, it was a different story. During the Khmer Rouge years, many had been elevated not because of ability, but because of their loyalty to Angkar. Now, with Angkar gone, they found themselves powerless again. They had land, but no animals to plow it. They had fields, but no tools or seeds. Survival required time, patience, and resources —things we did not have. In the countryside, life remained chaotic. We had to share what little we had just to stay alive until new systems could be built.

This contrast opened my eyes. I saw clearly that while material things can be stolen, burned, or lost to war, knowledge remains. Those who had it could rise again, even after years of hiding. Those without it, no matter how privileged they once were, struggled when the tide turned.

And here was the tragedy of the villagers—especially the young men and women who had been given privileges under the Khmer Rouge. Their "authority" had never been earned. It was not built on skill, education, or wisdom, but handed to them by Angkar to serve its purposes. When Angkar fell, so did their privileges. They were left empty-handed, lost in a world that suddenly required initiative and knowledge.

For nearly a decade—from the overthrow of Sihanouk in 1970 until the collapse of Pol Pot in 1979—Cambodia had been sealed off from the outside world. A whole generation of young villagers had grown up without education. Many were completely illiterate, including my younger brothers, who were six years younger than me. They had never had the chance to sit in a classroom, to hold a book, to write their own names. Their childhoods had been swallowed by war and labor. They lost not just years of learning, but the very foundation of how to think for themselves.

The New People, by contrast, had only lost about four years of education. Before 1975, many of them had been in school in the cities, studying until the Khmer Rouge took power. When the Vietnamese came, these survivors could pick up where they had left off, resuming their education and using their knowledge to rebuild their lives. It was not easy, but at least they had a starting point.

When freedom came, many of the New People gathered their families and returned to the cities where their houses still stood, where their businesses—though damaged—remained. They had connections, skills, and a framework to begin again. Shops reopened, schools filled with eager students, and the hum of life returned to the city streets. The scars of war were there, but the foundation for rebuilding had survived.

The Old People, however, especially the young men and girls who had grown up in the villages, carried nothing but the weight of tragedy. They had no schools to return to, no homes preserved, no businesses waiting for their hands. Their "education" had been years of forced labor in the fields, digging ditches, carrying soil, and watching friends and family die. Their minds had been trained in survival, not in learning. When freedom finally came, it exposed not opportunity but disadvantage.

For the villagers, the new society moved like a river they could not enter. The cities surged ahead with education and commerce, but the villagers stood at the shore, empty-handed. The cycle of poverty gripped them tighter than before, because now they were competing in a world that demanded skills they had never been allowed to gain. They were left behind—not by laziness, but by the cruel theft of their child-hood and youth.

And so I made a choice for myself. My family had no gold, no land, no hidden treasure. But I had my mind, and I had my will. I decided I would not waste this freedom drifting aimlessly. Too many of my friends wasted their days in empty celebrations, as if freedom was only for eating, drinking, and partying. I could not follow them.

I knew I must leave the village. If I wanted a new life, I would have to pursue it. Freedom meant opportunity, but opportunity required effort. Survival was no longer enough—I wanted to live with purpose.

Looking back, I realized that Pol Pot could kill bodies, burn books, and silence voices, but he could not destroy the hunger to learn. That hunger became my greatest treasure. It was knowledge—not diamonds, not land—that would shape my future.

The tide had turned for the New People. We rose again, scarred but standing. The Old People remained, struggling to find their place in a society that was rebuilding itself with new rules.

For me, the lesson was unforgettable: dictators can shatter lives, but they cannot kill the mind. And so I resolved—no matter how difficult the road ahead— that I would keep learning. Because knowledge was the seed of life, no tyrant could steal. The greatest wealth is not what can be taken from you, but what is planted in your mind.

35

THE FALL OF THE KHMER ROUGE

A NEW GOVERNMENT INSTALLED

THE KHMER ROUGE rose to power by judging people not by wisdom or skill, but by how well they could bend to labor. A man's worth was measured in rice planted, in sweat poured, in obedience shown—even if he was starving. Intelligence, learning, or vision for the future meant nothing. How could a country expect to survive when its leaders valued brute labor above all else? Cambodia under Pol Pot was a nation designed for self-destruction.

The fall of the Khmer Rouge was, to me, nothing less than an act of God's grace. Without that intervention, Cambodia would have slipped into a dark society with no hope of a future. The new leaders who stepped in were far from perfect, but at least they had some common sense. They were men who could see beyond the rice fields, even if they were still uncertain of the path forward.

For me, a young man who had endured nearly ten years of suffering, the future was a mystery. Freedom was now ours, but it came with new fears. Under Angkar, the danger was always death. Now, the danger was survival in a society turned upside down.

The world around us had no currency. The Khmer Rouge had destroyed all money, so in its place came a strange market of trade. Gold, silver, and precious metals became the medium of exchange. A bracelet could buy a sack of rice. A small piece of silver could buy meat, fruit, or cloth. Rice itself became as valuable as money.

But this new system also bred corruption. Without a moral compass, people did whatever they could to survive. The rich grew richer, using what they had to gain even more, while the poor slid deeper into desperation. For villagers, survival depended on the land passed down from generations before. But once a man sold his land, it was gone forever. Poverty followed, and there was no safety net to catch him.

For me, the struggle to survive pushed me to try new things. I planted tobacco by the lake, hoping it would give me something to trade. When I harvested and sold it, I managed to earn a small bit of gold. But even before that, I had taken a risk I should not have taken.

During one of the riots, when villagers rose against their leaders, many Khmer Rouge fled in panic. In the chaos, I saw an abandoned bicycle. Something inside me acted almost without thinking. I dismantled it, piece by piece, and buried it deep in the ground. It was a compulsive act—one that could have cost me my life if I had been caught. Angkar did not forgive theft, even of things left behind.

Months later, after I sold my tobacco harvest, I remembered that hidden treasure. I dug it up, cleaned it, and oiled the rusted chain. Piece by piece, I rebuilt it, and suddenly I had something priceless: transportation. With that bicycle, I could ride to the Thai border, buy goods, and bring them back to sell in the Cambodian market.

It was a dangerous trade. The Khmer Rouge still haunted the frontier, and every trip carried the risk of being caught, robbed, or killed. But to me, it was survival. I did not see it then as greed or ambition—it was simply the chance to live another day, to carve out a path in a world that had taken everything from us.

Looking back now, I realize how fragile my choices were. I had risked my life for material gain, for a piece of metal with two wheels. Yet in those years, even something as small as a bicycle could mean the difference between hunger and survival.

In those days, even survival tools carried danger. A bicycle should have been nothing more than a simple machine, but in Pol Pot's Cambodia, it became a secret, a risk, a gamble with life itself. One wrong move, one suspicious glance, and I could have been executed for daring to claim what had been abandoned.

That bicycle carried me farther than I ever thought possible—across fields, to the markets, and even toward the Thai border. Yet the more I look back, the more I see that my true survival did not rest on two wheels or the gold I earned from trading tobacco. Those things could be stolen, broken, or lost. What endured was something greater: the will to keep moving forward, the hunger to learn, the refusal to waste the life that had been spared.

Cambodia had fallen into ruin, but within me rose a quiet conviction: knowledge, not possessions, would be the true wealth of my future. I had survived brutality, deception, and fear. Now I had to learn how to survive freedom.

In the first weeks after the collapse of Pol Pot's regime, life felt unreal. The silence that had once choked the land was suddenly broken by laughter, music, and reckless celebration. For the first time in years, we could speak freely, eat without ration, and walk without fear. My friends and I partied through the nights, drinking and singing as if every day might be our last. We had lived too long in death's shadow, and this sudden freedom felt like a dream we did not want to wake from.

But after a few weeks of this wild living, the emptiness began to sink in. One morning, I woke up and realized how foolish I had been. I had endured years of suffering, hunger, and loss—yet here I was, wasting the very life I had fought so hard to keep. It was as if I had survived the storm only to drown in calm waters.

That was when I went to my mother and asked if she had any gold or savings left—something we could use to start a new life. Her answer broke my heart. She looked at me with quiet sorrow and said she had nothing left. Everything was gone—our home, our possessions, our family's small wealth—all consumed by the years of war and oppression.

In that moment, something in me changed. I realized that no one was coming to rescue us, that the future we hoped for would not be handed to us—we had to build it ourselves. I made the decision to leave quietly, without telling my friends. I knew they would try to stop me, content to live in the illusion of joy while the world around them still lay in ashes. But I could not stay. I had to move forward.

Around me, the contrast could not have been sharper. Many of my neighbors and friends—those who under

Pol Pot had once enjoyed privilege and power—now found themselves lost. They had been elevated not by merit, but by the regime's design, handed authority without wisdom or compassion. When Angkar fell, that borrowed power vanished overnight. With no guidance, no skills, and no purpose, many turned to drinking, gambling, and despair. They had survived the Killing Fields, only to become prisoners of their own freedom. Watching them, I understood how dangerous liberty could be when the mind was still enslaved.

I came to realize that freedom itself must be carried with care. It is not simply the absence of chains; it is the presence of discipline, responsibility, and a heart willing to do what is right. In a world left in chaos, freedom demanded protection—through patience, through learning, through the courage to rebuild one small step at a time.

Many could not bear that burden. The fields that once yielded grain now lay barren, for the seeds were gone and the will to plant had withered. The long years of terror had stripped people of hope, leaving them too weary to begin again. To some, this new freedom felt like another curse—a cruel reminder of what had been lost and what could never return.

But for me, it was different. I chose not to measure my life by what I lacked, but by what I still had—the gift of breath, the chance to learn, the freedom to move forward. I resolved to walk into the unknown future, not as a victim of the past, but as a student of its lessons.

Looking back now, I see that my survival was no accident. The same God who preserved me through the darkness also gave me light for the road ahead. He taught me that true freedom is not just being released from oppression—it is learning to live with wisdom, humility, and gratitude for every new beginning.

And so, as my country struggled to rise from its ruins, I began to rebuild my own life—step by step, lesson by lesson—trusting that even in the aftermath of destruction, God could still make something new.

36
EXILED IN TEARS
THE REFUGEE TRAIL TO THAILAND

THE ROAD to Thailand was long and treacherous. I had traveled it many times before on my bicycle, joining groups of traders who made the dangerous journey to buy goods and carry them back into Cambodia. Each trip took nearly a week, back and forth, and every time we knew the risks. Bandits hid along the smuggler's route, waiting for traders to return heavy with goods. Many were killed, their hard-earned supplies stolen in an instant. Death lurked on that trail like a shadow, but for those of us who had nothing, the risk felt like the only option.

It was along this path that my life began to change. My cousins asked me to help guide them to the Thai border. They had survived the Khmer Rouge, but like so many others, they were desperate to leave Cambodia. Thailand had become a passageway to something unimaginable—a chance at a new life in the third countries opening their doors to refugees. I agreed to take them, since I was traveling that way anyway.

When we reached the border, I expected to part ways. My plan was simple: trade, buy what I needed, and return home. Cambodia, even with all its pain and scars, was still my home. I had no thought of leaving it. But my cousins offered me to go with them to the refugee camp set up by the United Nations, but I thanked them for their kindness and did not take their offer. For the first time, the world had turned its eyes to Cambodia. After the fall of Pol Pot, the horrors of the Killing Fields became known, and humanitarian aid began to pour in. The refugee camps along the Thai border became sanctuaries of survival, places where the broken and displaced could gather, waiting for a chance to start again.

I left them at the camp and returned home. I carried my goods, and in my heart I carried a sense of relief that I had done my part. Leaving Cambodia was not an option for me—I could not imagine abandoning my homeland, even though I had been branded an outcast under the Khmer Rouge. Besides, I did not want to burden others with my survival.

But then word came. My cousins sent for my aunt, my mother's sister, to join them at the camp. She had always been kind and generous, a woman of compassion. Before she left Cambodia for good, she extended an invitation to me and to my brothers—David, Andrew, and Tony. She wanted us to come with her, to leave behind the soil of Cambodia and step into the unknown.

The road to Thailand was not a road at all—it was a scar, carved deep into the land by years of war. Every block along the main highway had been ripped apart by bombs or trenches, cut deliberately for battle. To cross, we had to balance thin sheets of plywood over the gaping holes. Each step felt like a gamble, as though the ground itself could give way beneath us.

All around were reminders that the war had not ended so neatly. Buildings stood in ruin—walls cracked, roofs collapsed, their skeletons reaching into the sky as monuments to destruction. The earth itself was littered with the bones of the dead, some not yet properly buried, scattered and half-covered by dust and weeds. It was as if the land groaned with the weight of untold stories, each ruin whispering of lives cut short.

Even in the silence, death was never far. The war had ended, but its echoes still claimed lives. Sometimes, an old unexploded bomb would detonate without warning —a sudden thunder that shook the ground and sent fear rippling through the villages. Each time, the news followed: another innocent life lost, not to battle, but to the remnants of it. Liberation had come, but peace had not yet arrived. The land itself seemed poisoned, every step haunted by the past.

During the years of conflict, both sides had filled the countryside with landmines—hidden killers buried in rice fields, paths, and forests. They were laid to stop enemies from advancing, but after the war, no one knew exactly where they were. The maps were lost, the soldiers who placed them long gone. And so, the danger remained.

Every day brought new casualties. Villagers who went to the forest to gather wood, or children who wandered too far from home, could vanish in an instant. The sound of explosions became a cruel reminder that the war's shadow still lingered in our soil. Many families lived in constant fear—not of soldiers anymore, but of the ground beneath their feet.

Even years later, the wounds continued. The remnants of Pol Pot's resistance still roamed in hiding, planting new mines to disrupt the fragile peace and strike fear into the people. They had lost power, but not their hatred, and their vengeance continued to spill innocent blood.

I learned this pain in the most personal way. After I had left the country, news reached me that my third brother had been killed. He was driving a small passenger bus between towns when his vehicle struck a landmine buried by Pol Pot's remaining forces. In a single moment, his life—and the lives of many others —were gone.

That loss cut deep. It was a cruel reminder that even though I had escaped, the war had not released its grip on my family. My brother had survived the Killing Fields, only to be claimed by the very remnants of that nightmare. Cambodia was free in name, but still bleeding. The earth itself seemed to weep for its children— those who had survived the terror of Angkar only to fall to the invisible hands of its ruins. Truly, it was freedom bought with tears.

That was the world we lived in—one where even peace was lined with danger. The war had ended, yet its poison lingered beneath our feet. Every field, every road, every step carried the possibility of death. And still, we moved forward, because there was nothing left behind to hold us.

This was the trail we traveled, the so-called path to a new beginning. For me, it was both familiar and foreign. I had taken this road many times before, riding my bicycle with other traders, risking bandits and ambushes. It was known as the smuggler's route, and every trip carried the danger of being killed for what you carried back from Thailand. Survival was never guaranteed.

But now the road bore more than traders. Families with children, widows, the weak and weary—all walked the same path, their faces hollow with hunger, their eyes wide with fear and desperate hope. They were not traveling for trade, but for survival, fleeing in search of refuge across the border.

Among them was my aunt—my mother's sister. Before the war, she had been a wealthy woman in the city. She and my uncle had lived a life of comfort, raising their family with dignity and generosity. She was kind, respected, and always ready to help those in need. But when the Khmer Rouge came, her wealth became meaningless.

She endured the suffering of the *New People*, stripped of everything, forced into the fields like the rest of us. Along the way, she lost two of her sons and later her husband— my uncle. Their deaths broke her heart, but somehow she found the strength to survive. She pressed on, carrying her remaining children through those dark years.

When the opportunity came, she made the decision to leave Cambodia. She could not endure another turn of cruelty, nor could she risk losing the rest of her family. For her, leaving was not just survival—it was an act of love for the sons and daughters she still had.

Through her courage, a door opened. Her journey became the bridge for mine. What began as my effort to help her soon became the turning point of my own life. Her invitation to join the escape would change everything—and the refugee camp that awaited us would become the place where my future was planted.

37
SEEDS OF A NEW BEGINNING
LEARNING IN EXILE, DREAMING BEYOND CAMBODIA

THE REFUGEE CAMP was the first place I had known in years where I could sleep without the sound of gunfire or the endless slogans blaring from loudspeakers. For the first time, there was safety—though not yet peace in my heart.

Inside the camp, I tried to learn what I could about the world beyond Cambodia. People spoke of countries I had never imagined—France, Australia, Canada, America. Families applied to resettle in nations I barely knew existed. Most of those around me were from the cities. They had money, resources, and the knowledge to escape. For villagers like me, the camp felt like another planet. I was twenty-one years old, with no education behind me, no common stories to share when young people gathered. They spoke of schools, theaters, and city life. I had only the memories of rice fields, bomb shelters, and survival.

So I chose a different path. I decided to study.

The living conditions were far from ideal. We were placed on high ground in a remote part of Thailand. The weather was brutally hot, the air thick and humid, and each person received only three liters of water per day—a ration that had to serve for both drinking and washing. It was a place of hardship, but also a place of hope. In its barrenness, I began to learn patience, for the future was waiting beyond those dry hills.

In the beginning, I went to English lessons with three friends I had met in the camp. But after only a week, the heat and discomfort drove them away. They could not bear the conditions. I, however, could not allow my circumstances to deter me. For the first time in my life, I had a chance to learn freely, and I clung to it with everything in me.

I had saved a little gold from my trading, but I held it tightly. I did not know if I would ever make it to America—or anywhere. If I was forced back into Cambodia, that gold might be my only chance to begin again. Instead, I turned my attention to something no one could steal from me: learning.

For the first time in my life, I studied English. Missionaries came into the camp and offered free classes, and I eagerly joined. But I wanted more. In the camp, some Cambodians who had more education offered private lessons for a fee. I could not afford them, but I stood outside the classrooms made of palm leaves, listening through the walls. I copied words into my notebook, practicing until my hands cramped.

Each morning, I woke at three o'clock, long before the camp stirred. In those quiet hours, while others slept, I studied. During the day, I wrote down lines of English over and over, even if I did not yet understand them. My goal was simple: to train my hand and mind to hold knowledge.

To my surprise, I discovered a gift. I began tutoring family friends, teaching them the little English I knew. They loved it—and encouraged me to open my own class. It felt daring, even foolish, but I agreed. With bamboo, I built benches. I found a small board to use as a blackboard. Soon I had thirty students, children and adults, divided into two classes. I taught for three hours every day—one and a half hours for each group.

The small fees they gave me allowed me to finally pay for lessons inside the classroom instead of standing outside. If my students asked me something I didn't know, I would arrive early to my own class to ask the teacher, and then return with the answer. I was no longer only a listener in the shadows—I was a student, and also a teacher.

There were times, of course, when loneliness pressed heavy on me. I missed my home, my father's voice, my mother who still stayed behind in my old village, and my siblings scattered by war. Sometimes depression filled me like an emptiness I could not shake. In those moments, I walked to the hospital in the camp. Foreign doctors treated the sick and wounded, and when I saw their suffering, I was reminded of how blessed I was just to be alive and to have a chance to learn. It lifted my spirit, giving me the strength to return to my work.

This was the turning point of my life. Cambodia had taken my childhood, but here in exile, I found the seed of my future. Not gold. Not land. Not even safety. It was education—knowledge that could never be stripped away, never confiscated by Angkar, never lost to war.

And more than that, I realized it was not only my determination. It was the Creator Himself who had me in His mind, the One who gave me the ability to learn and to dream again. What I thought was a small seed in barren soil was in truth a gift planted by God. And when the conditions were right, that seed began to grow.

I left Cambodia in tears, carrying scars I would never forget. But in this refugee camp, I began to dream of something beyond survival. I began to dream of life.

Circumstances may limit your body, but they cannot imprison the seed of learning God plants in your soul.

38
THE RETURN OF THE KING
A SYMBOL OF HEALING

WHEN I SAW the news of the King's return, I was no longer in Cambodia. By then, I was in America, building a new life, working hard, raising my family, and embracing my new identity as an American citizen. Yet when I watched those images on the screen—the crowds filling the streets, the people waving flags, the tears of joy streaming down their faces—it touched something deep inside of me. Cambodia had never left my heart.

For decades, our country had suffered under the crushing weight of war, genocide, hunger, and brokenness. We had lost millions of lives, generations of potential, and the very trust that once bound our villages together. Seeing the King return was not just a political moment—it was a symbol of healing, of a nation finding a way to breathe again after years of suffocation.

I remembered the boy I had once been—the boy who had cheered when Sihanouk called, the boy who believed loyalty to him would save Cambodia. Later, I felt betrayed when his voice disappeared, and Angkar rose in his shadow. For years, I carried the weight of that disillusionment. But when I saw his return, I did not feel bitterness. I felt relieved. At last, Cambodia could begin to close one chapter and open another.

The people's joy was genuine. They danced, they sang, they wept. For many, it was the first time in years they had felt safe to celebrate anything. His presence gave them hope that Cambodia was not only a land of ruins and mass graves but a nation with roots deep enough to endure. The monarchy, despite its flaws, was something familiar, something that connected the living to their ancestors and to the culture that Pol Pot had tried to erase.

When Sihanouk returned on **14 November 1991**, after years of exile, the nation greeted him with tears of joy. Then, in 1993, after Cambodia's first democratic elections under United Nations supervision, he was reinstated as King under a new constitutional monarchy. His role was no longer one of political power but of moral authority. As head of state, he became a unifying figure—ratifying laws, opening sessions of government, receiving diplomats, and reminding the people of their identity. In those fragile years of rebuilding, he gave Cambodia something priceless: continuity and dignity. His return was not about ruling, but about healing.

For me, watching from afar gave me a sense of closure. I had moved on with my life in America, and God had blessed me with new beginnings. But part of my heart was still Cambodian, still tied to the soil where my parents were buried and where so many of my people had suffered. To see the King return was to feel that Cambodia, wounded though it was, still had life in it.

It reminded me that healing is possible, even after unthinkable loss. Cambodia would never be the same, and neither would I. But joy could grow again in the places where sorrow had once taken root.

The streets of Phnom Penh echoed with cheers that day, and though I was thousands of miles away, I felt them in my chest. Cambodia had suffered enough. Now, at last, it was beginning to heal.

The King returned to his throne, but more importantly, Cambodia returned to itself.

39
JUSTICE SERVED
THE SILENCE OF A TYRANT

WHEN I FIRST HEARD THE news that Pol Pot had been captured in June of 1997, it felt unreal. For years, he had been a ghost in the jungles, a shadow name whispered but never seen. Suddenly, the man who had haunted our nation was no longer untouchable. The government declared it the end of the Khmer Rouge movement, both politically and militarily. For many Cambodians, it was as if a heavy weight had finally shifted.

But this was not the first time he had been judged. Back in 1979, the People's Revolutionary Tribunal in Phnom Penh had sentenced him to death in absentia. I remember hearing of it then, but it felt hollow. He was not there. His hands were never bound, his face never confronted the people whose lives he had destroyed. That verdict was more a symbol than a reckoning.

The real reckoning, I thought, would come when he stood before the people, when mothers and fathers could look him in the eye, when survivors could speak their truth. But that day never came. After his capture, he was placed under house arrest by his own comrades. He lived his last months not in chains, but in the relative quiet of the jungle, frail and old. On **April 15, 1998**, he died in his sleep. No trial. No confession. No apology.

When I heard of his death, my feelings were tangled. On one hand, there was relief—relief that his chapter was closed, that he could no longer command or deceive. On the other hand, there was sorrow. Not sorrow for him, but for the justice that was denied. He escaped the courtroom. He escaped the testimony of the people he had silenced. He escaped hearing the cries of those who lost their families, their homes, their very lives.

It felt, in some ways, unfinished. The man who had turned Cambodia into a prison, who had filled our land with bones, slipped away quietly without facing the world.

And yet, justice is not only in the courts. Justice is in memory. Justice is in the voices that refuse to be silenced. Justice is in the survivors who carried their stories, who rebuilt their lives, who dared to hope again. The trials that later convicted his lieutenants—Nuon Chea, Khieu Samphan, and others—were important. But the greater judgment was already written in the soil of Cambodia, in the mass graves that testified louder than any witness, in the tears of every survivor who lived to tell.

For me, it was a reminder that evil may run for a time, but it cannot hide forever. Its power always devours itself. Pol Pot was not captured by foreign armies or international courts, but by his own men, betrayed by the very system of paranoia and fear he created. That was his true judgment—he lived to see his empire crumble, his comrades turn against him, and his name become a curse.

When I think of him now, I do not see the strong leader he once pretended to be. I see a frail man carried in a hammock through the jungle, no longer feared, no longer followed, no longer in control. His end was small compared to the devastation he unleashed.

Cambodia still carries the scars, and justice will never feel complete. But his fall reminds us that no throne of terror stands forever.

The world said *"never again"* after the Holocaust. And yet, it happened again in Cambodia. But Pol Pot's death is a reminder that even the darkest tyrant cannot escape the hand of judgment.

He silenced millions, but in the end, it was silence that swallowed him.

And yet, here is my personal truth: I have been adopted by the King of kings, who poured out His grace upon me. Because of Jesus Christ, my Savior, I have chosen to forgive even Pol Pot. Not because he deserved it, but because I was forgiven first. For years, I carried the scar of suffering, and though I cannot erase it, I have learned to move forward in God's grace. What was once only pain has become a testimony I now use to help others.

Yes, it has taken years, and I am still learning, still growing stronger and healthier in Christ. But I know this: the grace of God is greater than the evil of man. Pol Pot tried to destroy life, but through God's mercy, my life has been redeemed. His scar remains, but it no longer defines me. It points me instead to the One who heals, and to the hope that even in the face of evil, grace has the final word.

Pol Pot's reign ended in silence, but my life continues in the song of grace.

EPILOGUE: FROM THE KILLING FIELDS TO FREEDOM

I have often asked myself why I survived when so many others did not. I was no stronger, no braver, no more deserving than the millions who perished. Yet my life was spared—again and again—through war, famine, forced labor, and the threat of execution. And I believe it was for a reason.

The Khmer Rouge tried to erase us. They tore down our temples, destroyed our schools, divided families, and filled the land with silence and bones. They told us we were nothing but tools—that if we were of no gain, we were of no use, and if of no use, we could be discarded.

But they were wrong.

Even in the darkest hours, I learned that the human spirit cannot be erased so easily. In the refugee camp, when I picked up a piece of chalk and began to teach, I discovered something Pol Pot could not kill: the hunger to learn, the desire to live, and the will to keep moving forward.

I share my story because memory itself is a form of resistance. Forgetting would be surrendering twice—once to the regime that tried to destroy us, and again to silence. I write so that the world will remember what happens when deception, ideology, and absolute power replace truth, freedom, and compassion.

My story is not only about Cambodia. It is also a warning. Evil often comes quietly, with promises of equality, with slogans of a better tomorrow. But step by step, it strips away freedom, family, and faith, until nothing is left but fear.

And yet, even in the midst of such darkness, there was grace. I was spared. I was given the chance to live, to learn, and to tell. Years later, when I saw the King return to his people, I realized that even nations can heal. The cheers in the streets of Phnom Penh were not only for a man—they were for dignity restored, for memory reclaimed, for a people who had suffered too long. And when I heard of Pol Pot's capture, and later his death, I felt a strange closure. Justice in this world was incomplete, but I had already found a greater justice. I had been adopted by the King of kings, whose grace healed my scars and taught me to forgive even the man who had brought so much suffering.

I am forever grateful to America—the nation that opened its arms and gave me a home when I had none. Here, I was free not only to live, but to dream, to learn, to build, and to pursue the true happiness that once seemed impossible in the shadows of Cambodia. America became the soil where the seed of my survival could finally grow into a life of meaning.

And above all, I am thankful to Jesus Christ, my Savior. In Him, I found not only survival, but identity. He adopted me into His family, gave me a future when I saw none, and placed in me a hope that no regime, no war, and no suffering could destroy. His grace was the anchor of my life in the Killing Fields, and His promise remains the foundation of my future.

To the reader of this book: cherish freedom. Guard it carefully. Value knowledge, because it cannot be stolen. And never take the dignity of another human life lightly. For I know, from the fields of Cambodia, that once dignity is stripped away, destruction soon follows.

This book is not only my story. It is the voice of the voiceless. It is the memory of those who cannot speak. And it is my offering of hope—that from the ashes of horror, life can rise again.

The Killing Fields wrote scars on my body, but God's grace wrote freedom on my soul.

Made in the USA
Columbia, SC
06 March 2026

39584a3d-2f93-457f-a474-e0310e795348R01